D1732697

Seeds of Success

Entrepreneurship and Youth

William B. Walstad • Marilyn L. Kourilsky

KENDALL/HUNT PUBLISHING COMPANY
4050 Westmark Drive   Dubuque, Iowa 52002

CONTENTS

LIST OF TABLES

ACKNOWLEDGMENTS

The authors would like to thank Kelly Brine for his inspired chapter illustrations. We would also like to express our appreciation to Kurt Mueller, president of the Kauffman Center for Entrepreneurial Leadership, and Greg Kourilsky, computer technologist, for their invaluable advice and counsel. Additional thanks go to Carol Allen, Gary Heisserer, Pam Hinderliter, Kate Pope Hodel, Sharon Nemeth, Daniel Buchheit and Ken Rebeck for their assistance in bringing this book to press. Finally, we would like to acknowledge the support provided by the staff at the Gallup Organization.

FOREWORD

From the lemonade stand up the street to the burgeoning stream of commerce on the information super-highway, the signs are all around us: entrepreneurship continues to be a driving force in shaping America's economy. Less obvious are the influences that encourage certain young people to become entrepreneurs while others choose more traditional career paths. Among his strong passions in the worlds of entrepreneurship and philanthropy, Ewing Marion Kauffman cared deeply about youth having the option to become entrepreneurs and to engage in entrepreneurial thinking in all aspects of their lives. That passion was shared by the team that founded the Kauffman Center for Entrepreneurial Leadership at the Ewing Marion Kauffman Foundation and has permeated the mission of the Kauffman Center as it seeks creative approaches to accelerate entrepreneurship in the United States.

Are informed choices being made by America's youth? Do entrepreneurial role models exist within their families or communities? What do young people really know about the advantages and disadvantages of being one's own boss? Does our current educational system impart the right information and guidance—at the right times—to optimize entrepreneurial potential? These are just a few of the important questions researched and discussed by Marilyn and Bill in *Seeds of Success*.

Clearly, the results presented in this book emphasize the importance of entrepreneurship to young people today. A surprisingly large majority wants to start their own businesses, primarily because they wish to control their own destinies. Just as clearly, these same results bring into sharp relief that youth are not prepared to embark on the entrepreneurial endeavors they hope to pursue in such large numbers. Those who do not learn about entrepreneurship "at the dinner table" typically do not perceive that they have access through their schooling to the skills and knowledge that would enable them to have a full-fledged shot at "making a job" rather than "taking a job." Mr. Kauffman did not live to see the results of the landmark research contained in this book. However, I am confident it would have reinforced his opinion about the importance of the Kauffman Center's work in exposing youth to the exciting potential of both entrepreneurship and entrepreneurial thinking for enhancing their lives.

As you read the following chapters, I encourage you to use them as stepping stones to further discussion and action with respect to enhancing the role of entrepreneurial thinking and entrepreneurship in the education and everyday lives of America's youth. The leadership team and associates of the Kauffman Center believe, as did Mr. Kauffman, that introducing young people to the opportunity and excitement of entrepreneurship is critical both to their success and to the future health of our communities. I hope that the results of this research will encourage you to join us in our efforts. We believe that our youth deserve no less than the knowledge and self-concept that would provide them the option of building their own future by identifying creative opportunities and pursuing them in the face of uncertainty.

Michie P. Slaughter
Founding president, retired
Kauffman Center for Entrepreneurial Leadership
at the Ewing Marion Kauffman Foundation

IGNITING THE SPARK:

Entrepreneurship in America

Each year, thousands of new businesses are started. We are all familiar with them, especially those located in our immediate community. The dry cleaner, the auto repair shop and the home construction company are common examples. Although these businesses may remain relatively small, they deliver valuable products and services for the community year after year—and employ many people in the local economy.

Many of these small businesses survive and prosper. Some, especially those involved in developing new products, services or technology, eventually become larger corporations. A few even become very large; consider the growth of Intel and Microsoft over the past few decades.

At the other end of the spectrum, however, are small businesses begun with great expectations—perhaps even great ideas—which, for one reason or another, fail to survive in the marketplace. In such cases, although entrepreneurial dreams and aspirations are severely challenged, all is not lost. The unsuccessful attempt to start a business and pursue a dream may be the initial test of an idea or a product that at a later time, under different circumstances or in the hands of another entrepreneur, may prove successful and profitable.

In an ironic way, then, business failure teaches valuable lessons even as it depletes financial and other resources. The education and experience gained is frequently used by the original entrepreneur or someone else at another time to create a successful business. In fact, the bankruptcy of a new business can be viewed as the tuition that is paid by individuals and society for an education that allows entrepreneurs to test new ideas and use that experience to achieve success in later years.

Shaking Up the Status Quo

Virtually every aspect of our society is permeated by the impact of entrepreneurial ventures. They create new products and services, trigger advances in technology, and are a constant source of competitive pressure on existing businesses to improve pricing, quality and function. Entrepreneurship also provides individuals opportunities to participate in and contribute to our economy, no matter what their gender, race, ethnicity, religion, education, income or country of origin.

Moreover, entrepreneurship "shakes up" the status quo of business and society by encouraging continual change. Joseph Schumpeter colorfully terms it "creative destruction." As the entrepreneur recognizes market opportunities and creates new products and technologies to meet them, older businesses that may have been resting on their laurels and market share are forced either to adapt to the new competition or step aside as customers express new preferences. In this way, entrepreneurship contributes over the long term to the emergence of successful challengers to the social and economic control exerted by concentrations of "old" wealth and power.

Entrepreneurship is also a significant contributor to the welfare of individuals and their communities beyond providing new employment opportunities and an expanded tax base. After all, most foundations throughout the country with major leadership roles in philanthropy were initially endowed by entrepreneurs who had amassed wealth through the success of the entrepreneurial ventures they had conceived and initiated.

Focusing on Youth

This book, however, is not a paean to the entrepreneur; a "how to" book about starting your own business; a personal finance book about creating wealth; or a sociological study of factors affecting business success or the causes of business failure. It is not a book about great entrepreneurs of history, a psychological look at how they behave or an inspirational book on what they think. It is not even a book about the economics of entrepreneurship. Many books have already been written on these subjects, and there is no need to duplicate their insights.

The central topic here is different, yet equally important: the investigation of the entrepreneurial spark in our nation's youth. While most studies look at entrepreneurship only after people have become entrepreneurs, or study a group in its prime years for entrepreneurship (ages 24 to 40), the focus of this book is the youth of our nation, ages 14 to 19 years.

Why? Because, given the accelerating importance of entrepreneurship from both an economic and a social perspective, youth attitudes, knowledge and skills with respect to the entrepreneurial process take on strategic significance. This younger cohort constitutes the primary pool from which the entrepreneurs and entrepreneurial thinkers of tomorrow must emerge—and a few are already on their way. In addition, access and equity issues associated with youth's capacity to participate successfully in the economy are increasingly linked to these same attitudes, knowledge and skills.

Naturally, not all teenagers become entrepreneurs. The careers they select are as varied as the many influences upon them, including personal preferences, home and family environments, education, and changing social and economic trends. Some may always work for someone else, or begin careers that way and then decide to start their own businesses. Others may start businesses that they operate in addition to their other employment.

Even those working for someone else, however, will find an increasing need for entrepreneurial thinking and behaviors to help their company and advance their careers. Consequently, we sought to integrate in this book the results of several threads of investigation into the fabric of a critical national resource—the entrepreneurship attitudes of our nation's youth (14 to 19) and their basic capacity to pursue entrepreneurial aspirations regardless of their career path.

Seeking Answers Step-by-Step

The foundations of our investigation were four major national Gallup surveys commissioned by the Kauffman Center for Entrepreneurial Leadership at the Ewing Marion Kauffman Foundation (the Kauffman Center) during the period 1994 to 1997. The item content, which formed the basis for the field survey instruments, was developed by a partnership between the Kauffman Center and the University of Nebraska. Key areas for which knowledge and attitudes were probed by the surveys included entrepreneurship, market economics, entrepreneurship education, small business operation and philanthropy.

The Gallup Organization, Inc. conducted all four surveys, selecting the national random samples, collecting data by telephone interview of respondents, and tabulating the survey data. The basic vehicle for our investigation was a survey that we prepared that contained a set of direct and uncomplicated questions for youth to answer. The responses to the questions and the implications to be drawn from them became the core content for the following chapters in this book.

Step one was to find out if youth were interested in starting a business. If so, why? If not, why not? The answers to these questions are found in Chapter 2. Because initiating a small business venture is a core ingredient of entrepreneurship, we were also interested in finding out what youth thought about small business compared to large corporations. Those perspectives and comparisons are reported in Chapter 3.

The next two chapters offer an assessment of youth's knowledge and opinions about entrepreneurship. In Chapter 4, we reviewed the results from a series of survey test questions to measure knowledge about basic topics in entrepreneurship and related understandings in economics. In Chapter 5, we sought their opinions on competitive markets and government because these views may influence the general climate for successful entrepreneurship and youth's capacity for success.

In Chapter 6, our attention turns to a subject that has been given little study: youth perspectives on philanthropy and entrepreneurship. Of particular concern are views on the contributions successful business owners make to the community. Did youth see the connection between business success and what the entrepreneur gives back to the community?

The focus of Chapter 7 is entrepreneurship education. The responses to our survey question that we report in this chapter reveal how youth perceived the business and economic education that they received in their schools. Finally, Chapter 8 presents some important implications from these studies of youth and entrepreneurship and offers concluding comments.

Expanding the Survey

This investigation also includes the results from administering the same survey questions to three adult groups during the course of the multiple surveys. The results for these other groups provide a basis for comparison, aiding in the interpretation of data.

We first wanted to know what youth thought relative to a sample of adults. To achieve this objective, we surveyed a sample of the general public that matched the U.S. Census Bureau's Current Population Survey for the adult population.

We also wanted to find out how youth responded to questions relative to a sample of teachers. To make this comparison, we surveyed a representative sample of all public and private teachers in grades 1-12 in the United States.

In addition, we thought it would be valuable to see the views youth held relative to a group that was more likely to understand more aspects of entrepreneurship: small business owners. To provide this contrast, we surveyed a representative sample of small business owners from a national data base of small businesses.[1] Seven in 10 of these businesses had fewer than 20 employees, and half had 10 or fewer employees.

Reporting the Results

As is the case for all surveys based on statistical sampling, the range of potential sampling error should always be kept in mind as one interprets results of the surveys reported and their potential significance. At the 95 percent level of confidence, the maximum expected range of sampling error for our major comparison groups varied from +/-2.4 percentage points for our largest samples to +/-6.9 percentage points for our smallest samples. For example, at the 95 percent level of confidence, the maximum expected range of sampling error for the sample of 1,008 youth that we surveyed was +/- 3.1 percentage points. This statement means that if 100 different samples of 1,008 youth were randomly chosen from the same national population, then 95 times out of 100 the sample results obtained would vary not more than +/- 3.1 percentage points from the results that would be obtained if the entire population of youth were surveyed. In fact, we found that the survey responses for this youth sample (n=1,008) are essentially the same, within the margin of sampling error, to those obtained a year earlier from another national random sample of youth (n=602) that have been widely reported.[2] We also found a .99 correlation between the responses to survey items for the two samples.

Sometimes the overall response from youth can mask significant differences based on selected characteristics. For example, the views of males and females can vary on important questions, as can those of blacks and whites. When we find these significant subgroup differences, we report them in the chapters that follow.[3] As you will discover, several of the differences are significant for the overall implications drawn.

One important caveat: not all of the responses or questions used in the survey are reported in the chapters that follow. The reason for not doing so was to spare the reader a great deal of the unnecessary detail and to be as parsimonious as possible in the selection and presentation of data, highlighting only the most important findings from the survey studies. More detailed information and the responses from each survey question can be found in previously published reports and studies.[4]

With this background, you are now ready to journey with us through the results. We believe you will find the journey revealing and well worth taking.

1. The final sample was a mix of small-business owners and managers. We did not split these groups because we saw little reason to do so. Seven in 10 of the group were small-business owners, so their views dominated the survey responses. The differences in the responses of the two groups were also very minor. For the sake of parsimony, we refer to this group as small-business owners throughout the text.

2. See Walstad (1994a) and/or Walstad and Kourilsky (1996).

3. The sample sizes for the subgroups are smaller and subject to greater sampling error than the total youth sample. Expected sampling error ranges were +/- 4.4% for the 490 females and +/- 4.5% for the 477 males. They were +/- 3.7% for the 713 whites, +/- 8.6% for the 129 blacks, and +/- 8.7% for the 126 Hispanics that were surveyed. Subgroup difference should be interpreted with caution.

4. See Walstad (1994a), Walstad (1996), Walstad and Kourilsky (1996), Kourilsky and Carlson (1997), Kourilsky and Esfandiari (1997), Kourilsky and Walstad (1998), Walstad and Kourilsky (1999).

LIVING THE DREAM:

Interest in Starting a Business

Imagine a world in which people are prevented from ever starting a business. The consequence of this economic policy would be an economy lacking the dynamism for technological change and the capacity for sustainable economic growth. In fact, the experiment has been tried a number of times, often leading to dismal results in the long run. A good example is the economic stagnation that existed in China before it adopted market reforms which encouraged entrepreneurship.

The economic experiment was different throughout the history of the United States, where there always has been ample opportunity for people to initiate business ventures. Economic freedom and entrepreneurship have been essential ingredients in the growth of the U.S. economy.

Thus, the "spirit of entrepreneurship" thrives as a vital part of the American dream. The belief that you can better yourself, improve the standard of living for your family, and control your destiny are central elements of that dream. Starting a business and making it successful often have been key avenues to the fulfillment of people's aspirations.

Is the Spirit Alive and Well?

What we sought to find out in our survey work was whether this spirit of entrepreneurship was alive and well in the minds of America's youth. Clearly, entrepreneurship often begins at an early age; even very young children have a strong desire for freedom and control to build something for themselves. Starting a business and running a business are natural offshoots of that inclination. The classic example of how this tendency gets directed into action is the "lemonade stand" businesses children start on hot summer days.

Of course, the desire for entrepreneurship goes well beyond the lemonade-stand business. There are numerous stories of young children already earning an income of their own from their entrepreneurial activity in areas ranging from pet-sitting services to detailing tractors.[1]

By the time those youth move into their teens, the avenues for entrepreneurship widen substantially because their capability for operating a business expands. Teenagers are able to identify opportunities and put a business plan into action that capitalizes on their insights. They also have the drive and energy to make a business succeed. There are many impressive examples of teens who have started companies and become successful.[2]

Challenging Conventional Wisdom

Naturally, not everyone is born with a desire to start a business. Many young people express other career aspirations, ranging from classic professions such as doctor, lawyer and engineer to careers in the arts and sciences, computers, agriculture and public service. However, they are commonly provided little exposure to the notion of starting a business or to the development of related business skills. Why? Because the conventional educational wisdom has been largely to ignore entrepreneurship and entrepreneurial thinking, instead of treating them as important components of career preparation.

This thinking is typified by the misguided notion that "doctors don't operate a business; they operate on people." If you look carefully at doctors as a group, they do indeed operate businesses. Increasingly, creating and sustaining a successful medical practice requires entrepreneurial acumen as well as medical skills (ask your doctor about it next time you make a visit for a checkup!)

The same argument can be made for most other occupations. Although not everyone will leave high school and immediately start a business, over their lifetimes most people will run a business or need some entrepreneurial skills. Even public servants need a strong dose of entrepreneurial training because running for political office has strong similarities to starting and running a business. Once in office, a good politician also needs to know how to use entrepreneurial skills to make government work more efficiently and benefit more people.

Less-Than-Great Expectations

When we started this study, we did not anticipate that the entrepreneurial aspirations of youth would be particularly high. Although it is clear some youth are interested in entrepreneurship—and we were familiar with many examples of youth starting and running a business—we did not believe the experience was widespread. In fact, we would have been surprised if more than one teenager in 10 were to say they were interested in starting a business; a figure that high would represent an impressive percentage of the nation's youth.

Why the initial pessimism? First, we perceived that parents and the media do little to encourage entrepreneurship and may even discourage it. After all, few parents are likely to say to their children, "I want you to grow up and start a business." They're more apt to say, "I want you to grow up and become a doctor" (or some other type of professional).

Second, the entertainment media only serve to reinforce the notion that there is something wrong with people who run their own businesses. Entrepreneurs are often portrayed as villains or criminals in television shows or movies. Given these examples, why would young people be interested in starting a business?

Third, most schools do little to encourage entrepreneurship, probably because they themselves are not encouraged to be entrepreneurial institutions. There are few entrepreneurial role models or experiences for learners, and teachers are often unfamiliar with how businesses are initiated or operated. Only scant attention is paid in school curricula to entrepreneurship education. School counselors frequently do not consider "becoming an entrepreneur" as a career, and are often more comfortable talking with youth about preparing for college to be trained to work for someone else.

Discovering an Untapped Reservoir

What we learned from our survey was that youth have a view of entrepreneurship that was much more positive than we had ever expected. When we asked youth, "Do you think you would want to start a business of your own?" almost seven in 10 said yes.[3]

These results are highly significant. This interest in entrepreneurship is an untapped reservoir with the potential to directly affect standards of living and the economy. If just a third of the youth who expressed an interest in starting a business actually acted on their aspirations at some point over their lifetimes, such initiative could significantly increase new business formation in the United States!

Further, even those who do not start businesses may be able to use their entrepreneurial drive to enhance careers and raise the standard of living for their families. The economy also can benefit from increased entrepreneurial activity: it increases productivity, reduces inflation, and contributes to long-term economic growth.

TABLE 2.1: Interest in Starting a Business of Your Own

Response	Youth (n=1,008)	General Public (600)	Teachers (1,609)
	%	%	%
Yes	65	50	54
No	31	49	45
Don't know	3	1	1

Exploring Older Groups

Our survey of the general public revealed that there was also strong interest in entrepreneurship among this group. We found that five in 10 members of the general public surveyed said they were interested in starting a business of their own. This high percentage is impressive, given that the average age of the sample was 44 years, and it easily could be assumed that interest in entrepreneurship would decline as people near retirement.

In fact, further investigation supported this assumption. Breaking the sample at the mean age produced a significant difference in response. Almost seven in 10 (66%) of those in the general public who were 25-44 years old (the prime age for entrepreneurship) were interested in starting a business. This percentage is about the same as found in the youth samples. By contrast, among those 45-64 years old, only about four in 10 (41%) expressed an interest in entrepreneurship. This percentage was still sizable, but lower relative to the younger members of the general public. Among those 65 years of age or older, interest in entrepreneurship fell to less than two in 10 (17%).

Elementary, My Dear Researcher

One might not expect those individuals established in a profession to be interested in starting a business because they have ostensibly already made a career decision. If the professional group were teachers, expectations might be even lower, considering their choice to work in the relatively non-entrepreneurial school structure. These speculations, however, did not hold for the national sample of teachers who were surveyed.

The interest in entrepreneurship that we found among teachers was similar to that found among the general public, with more than half of the teachers expressing an interest in starting a business. The average age of the sample was 44 years, or similar to the average age for the general public. A further breakdown of this sample by the mean age of the teacher revealed only minor differences in the interest expressed by older and younger teachers (53% versus 61%).

What appeared to be most important in predicting teacher interest in entrepreneurship was the grade level at which the teacher taught. A significantly greater percentage of secondary teachers (58%) were interested in starting a business than were elementary teachers (45%). Among elementary teachers, intermediate teachers were significantly more interested in starting a business than were primary teachers (49% versus 37%). Thus, teacher interest in entrepreneurship appears to rise with the age of students taught. The reason for this trend may have something to do with the more prescribed curriculum in elementary grades, as opposed to the greater opportunity secondary teachers enjoy in designing and running their own courses—something more similar to starting and running a business.

Moreover, teacher interest in entrepreneurship varied predictably according to the subject matter taught. Among middle school/junior high teachers, business educators were more interested in starting a business than were social studies teachers (68% versus 57%). Among senior high teachers, business educators showed more interest in starting a business (60%) than did social studies teachers (51%) or teachers of language arts, science or mathematics (49%).

Given their career interest in business and education, it certainly stands to reason business teachers would be the most entrepreneurially inclined of all teacher groups. The question, however, is whether their students ever get the opportunity to benefit from this entrepreneurial enthusiasm. The school curriculum is structured in such a way that relatively few students receive an effective business or entrepreneurship education—an issue which will be discussed in Chapter 7.

Bridging the Gender Gap

Between 1987 and 1992, the growth of women-owned businesses outpaced the overall growth of businesses by nearly two to one. The growth in sales generated by women-owned businesses also exceeded the overall growth of businesses by nearly two to one. One-third of businesses now are owned by women, and they employ one out of every four workers in the United States.[4]

These developments motivated our interest in entrepreneurship among female youth. Was there strong interest that would continue to fuel the significant trend toward women ownership of businesses in the U.S. economy? The answer from our survey was clearly, "Yes!" The great majority of female youth—more than six in 10 (61%)—were interested in starting a business of their own. Fewer than four in 10 (35%) were not interested in starting a business. These results suggest there is a large potential pool of female youth who may decide to choose a career path in entrepreneurship, increasing the number of women-owned businesses.[5]

The survey results also showed female youth to be significantly less likely than males to want to start a business of their own. Among youth, about one in 10 more males than females were interested in starting a business (70% versus 61%).[6]

The reason for this male-female gap is difficult to explain. There were no detectable differences in male-female knowledge of entrepreneurship among youth that would account for the difference, as we will report in Chapter 4, although knowledge of entrepreneurship was low in both male and female groups. Other findings we will report showed females were more aware of their knowledge deficiencies than were males—a fact that may make them less confident in their ability to succeed in starting a business.

From the opposite perspective, males may have been overly confident of their abilities, given their actual level of knowledge. There also may be teaching or curricular practices that reduce the level of  female interest in starting a business. Whatever the reason for this difference, the topic merits further study because it directly affects the size of the pool of female entrepreneurs.

Ethnicity and Entrepreneurship

Because the United States has been experiencing significant growth in black entrepreneurship in recent years, the youth responses also were studied for important differences by ethnicity. One indicator of this trend is the change in the number of black-owned businesses. From 1987 to 1992, the number of black-owned businesses increased by 46 percent. By contrast, the total number of firms increased just 26 percent. Black-owned businesses also experienced substantial growth during the period, with sales and receipts rising by 63 percent, compared with a 50-percent increase for all firms.[7]

The data also show that the number and size of black-owned firms are still relatively small and that they employ few workers. In 1992, they represented only 3.6 percent of all firms and accounted for approximately one percent of sales and receipts.

Also, only 10 percent of these firms had employees, although they generated 70 percent of the sales and receipts for all black-owned firms.[8] With the growth of our economy increasingly relying on entrepreneurship, these data indicate the need for more participation by black Americans. This is essential if they are to own businesses, generate revenues, and create jobs in relative percentages more consistent with their demographic presence in the U.S. population.

What we found was a very strong interest in entrepreneurship among black youth. Specifically, three-fourths of black youth said they were interested in starting a business. This percentage was significantly higher than that for either whites (63%) or Hispanics (64%). These results suggest there is a large potential pool of entrepreneurs among blacks, even at a young age. The key problem is ascertaining how to tap into this pool and expand black entrepreneurship in the United States.

Pinning Down Positive Motivations

We wanted to explore the motivation of the seven out of 10 youth who wanted to start a business of their own. What reason do you think they would give for undertaking such a project? Would it be to earn lots of money and become rich? Would it be to be their own bosses? Would it be to give themselves a challenge to overcome? Would it be to build something for the community or the family? We posed this question to the youth in our sample who expressed an interest in starting a business.

Being Your Own Boss. We found the reason most youth gave for wanting to start a business had something to do with a strong desire for independence and control. More than four in 10 offered variations on the independence or control theme with such reasons as "To be my own boss," "To do what I want to do," "Just to have my own business," "To be independent," "For control," "To control my destiny," "Job security," or "For freedom." For a simple reference point, we'll use the most frequent response: "To be my own boss."

The responses of youth were similar to two adult groups who were asked about their reasons for being interested in starting a business. Among the general public who wanted to start a business, about five in 10 who were interested in doing so stated the desire, "To be my own boss." Among those teachers who expressed an interest in starting a business, more than four in 10 cited similar reasons for why they'd like to become entrepreneurs.[9]

TABLE 2.2: Reasons for Wanting to Start a Business*

Response	Youth (n=658)	General Public (300)	Teachers (870)
	%	%	%
A. To be my own boss	41	51	43
B. To earn lots of money	21	14	18
C. To use my skills and abilities	8	6	16
D. To overcome a challenge	7	9	12
E. To give back to community	7	5	5
F. To build something for the family	5	7	2
G. Other	5	7	5
H. Don't know	4	1	0

Only those who responded "Yes" to wanting to start a business

Discounting Money Matters. Given the common fare in television shows and the news media, one might assume "the pursuit of money" or "greed" as primary motives for why people want to be in business for themselves. Our survey results, however, showed very limited support for this stereotype of the business owner. The desire to become rich may be why people buy lottery tickets, but it was not the major motivating reason for starting a business among any of the groups surveyed. Only two in 10 youth thought earning lots of money was the primary reason why they'd want to become an entrepreneur.[10]

The low level of interest in money as the primary reason for entrepreneurship was also apparent among other groups. Even smaller percentages of the general public or teachers cited earning lots of money as a reason for their personal interest in starting a business.

Youth gave many other reasons for their interest in entrepreneurship, expressing a desire for personal development or philanthropy rather than simply being motivated by the desire for money. The reasons given were "To use my skills and abilities," "To overcome a challenge," "To build something for the family," or "To help the community." These are primarily non-pecuniary, and some might even say laudatory, reasons. Added up, the percentages account for more than a quarter of youth responses. Combined with the percentage who said they want "to be my own boss," a total of seven in 10 youth cited important *non-monetary* reasons for why they would like to start a business.[11]

Revealing Other Reasons. Our findings from the youth sample on other reasons are fairly similar to responses we found from the general public or teachers. Over a quarter of the general public gave the responses, "To use my skills and abilities," "To overcome a challenge," "To build something for the family," or "To help the community" as their reasons for entrepreneurship. Over a third of teachers gave one of those responses. In fact, about as many teachers cited "To use my skills and abilities" as "To earn lots of money" as their primary interest in entrepreneurship.

The major point is that the primary reasons that people want to go into business for themselves—youth or adults—are the strong desire to control their lives or to improve something: themselves, their family or their community. Becoming wealthy is a minor consideration. The stereotypical equating of the desire for entrepreneurship with the desire for money gives a distorted view of the entrepreneur.

Nailing Down the Negatives

We were equally curious about the reasons for not wanting to start a business among the three in 10 youth who expressed such reluctance. Our intent in probing further among the negative respondents was to see if we could identify potential barriers or misperceptions about entrepreneurship that could steer some youth away from considering this option for their lives. If these barriers are not addressed at an early age, then entrepreneurship is an option that may be dismissed from a person's thinking.

TABLE 2.3: Reasons for Not Wanting to Start a Business*

Response	Youth (n=316)	General Public (300)	Teachers (722)
	%	%	%
A. Lack of energy/time/skills/ideas	28	14	27
B. Like current education/job/ work situation	19	6	25
C. Age (too young/old)	2	37	15
D. Too risky	16	10	13
E. Business problems	17	20	9
F. Not enough money	11	8	7
G. Other	5	4	4
H. Don't know	3	1	0

*Only those who responded "No" to wanting to start a business

Is Something Lacking? What we found was that many of these youth felt they lacked something perceived as necessary for becoming entrepreneurs. They said they lacked energy or time, knowledge or skill, an idea or innovation, or money. These statements were supplied by almost four in 10 youth who were not interested in starting a business. Another two in 10 were satisfied with their current work or educational situation and were not interested in changing it.

Running Hard. The other four in 10 gave reasons related to the difficulty of running a business. Of great concern to some youth were the various problems involved: managing people; handling government regulation; paying taxes; and dealing with the stress and pressure. They also thought running a business was too risky. The possibilities that you might not be successful, lose your money, and go bankrupt were daunting prospects for some.[12]

What's the Big Idea? What these results suggest is that entrepreneurship education has the potential to have a strong influence in overcoming the "lack of something" barriers that youth perceive as reasons for not wanting to start a business.

Perhaps the most serious barrier is the lack of an idea or innovation. Educators can help students recognize opportunities and possibilities, and encourage them to think creatively about what can be done to solve a problem or overcome a challenge. Once an idea is in place, it then becomes easier to motivate the individual to spend the time and energy on the project because there is now personal interest in making a change.

Even those who are satisfied with their current situation need to be reminded that the world of work is constantly changing: what your education prepared you for and/or what job you are in today may not be what is wanted tomorrow. The best security in the job market is knowing you can be your own boss if necessary. Obviously, not everyone will select this option—but just knowing more about entrepreneurship should provide more job insurance.

Solid entrepreneurship courses also help prepare students for operating a business. They can enable students to learn about ways to obtain financing as well as handle stress and risk. In this case, education builds in students the capability and confidence to overcome these traditional obstacles to starting a business.

Generalizing on the General Public. The reasons the general public gave for not starting a business, among the half who were not interested, were somewhat similar to those reported by youth: they felt they lacked something or liked their current situation. About half also cited problems with running a business, such as management problems, risk or the need for financial capital. Predictably, the major difference between the youth and general public reservations about becoming an entrepreneur was the age factor. Well over a third of the general public felt they were too old to start businesses of their own.

The reasons teachers gave for not starting a business, among the almost five in 10 who were not interested, were similar to those given by youth and the general public. The major reasons, cited by more than a quarter of respondents, were a lack of energy, time, skills or ideas. Another quarter said they were satisfied with their current situation. More than three in 10 cited problems with running a business—management, business risk and the need for financial capital. Some teachers were also concerned that they were too old, but this percentage was less than half that of the general public.[13]

These findings beg the question: What would the world have been like if these groups had had more exposure to entrepreneurship education in their formative years? Perhaps some of those obstacles would not have looked insurmountable.

What Advice Would You Give?

One other survey question supplied insights into what youth, the general public and small-business owners thought about entrepreneurship. We presented this scenario and questions: *What advice would you give to a person who wanted to start a business? Would you encourage them to start a business now, tell them to wait a few years and get more work experience, or discourage them from starting a business in favor of working for someone else?*

TABLE 2.4: Encourage Someone Wanting to Start Their Own Business?

Response	Youth (n=1,008)	General Public (600)	Teachers (204)
	%	%	%
Encourage	28	61	53
Wait	68	28	28
Discourage	3	5	12
Don't know/Refused	1	5	7

The answers were somewhat surprising. Although most youth were interested in starting a business, they were also fairly conservative when it came to giving advice to others on the topic. Only three in 10 would encourage someone to start a business now, while about six to seven in 10 would tell someone to wait.

This cautious stance should not be interpreted as weak support for entrepreneurship, because very few said they would discourage someone who wanted to start a business. The reason that caution was expressed was more likely due to a combination of factors.

First, most young people lack significant work experience that provides a realistic basis for understanding how business works and what contribution an individual can make. Second, youth may also lack the necessary skills and knowledge to feel confident about pursuing an entrepreneurial dream. Both factors suggest that more entrepreneurship education would be helpful in overcoming these initial reservations and in building confidence.

The responses of the general public were almost the direct opposite of those of youth. Six in 10 of the general public would encourage someone who wanted to start a business; only about three in 10 would tell them to wait. As was the case with youth, very few would discourage someone who wanted to start a business. The general public may be more assertive than youth about advising entrepreneurship for others, because more of them have work experience. Their life experiences may also help them understand that if you don't act on your dreams, you will never realize them (or at least have the satisfaction of knowing that you made the attempt).

We surveyed small-business owners on this question because we were interested in what they thought, given their business experiences. Most of this group held views similar to the general public but were a bit more cautious in their responses. About five in 10 would encourage a person who wanted to start a business. About three in 10 would tell someone to wait. The most surprising response was that this group had the largest percentage who said they would discourage someone who was interested in starting a business. The percentage is still low and probably arises from the frustrations some small-business owners experience in their work that they do not want others to face. Most small-business owners like their work choice and would recommend it to others who wanted to start their own business.

We also wondered whether youth held positive views of small businesses and appreciated their contributions to society. These issues are explored in the next chapter.

1. For other examples, see Bernstein (1992). For a discussion of the elementary school curriculum for entrepreneurship, see Kourilsky (1990) and Kourilsky and Carlson (1997).

2. For examples, see Modu (1996). For a discussion of the secondary school curriculum for entrepreneurship, see Kent (1990) and Kourilsky and Carlson (1997).

3. We are confident that these results are not an aberration or a sampling fluke. The percentage of youth who said they were interested in starting a business is essentially equivalent, within the margin of sampling error, to the result from another national survey of youth that we conducted. That survey also found that almost seven in 10 (65%) youth were interested in starting their own business.

4. The most recent year for which data were available was 1992. See U.S. Department of Commerce (1996a) and NFWBO (1996).

5. This interest in entrepreneurship was not restricted to female youth, nor was it an attribute associated with youthful enthusiasm. In the general public survey, more than four in 10 (42%) females expressed interest in starting a business. Also, more than half of female teachers (52%) expressed interest in entrepreneurship.

6. This gap seems to widen with age. Among a sample of youth and younger adults (ages 14-39), the gap moves toward almost two in 10 (64% versus 47%). This gap is similar in size to that found in a survey of the general public (59% versus 42%).

7. The most recent year for which data were available was 1992. See U.S. Department of Commerce (1996b).

8. U.S. Department of Commerce (1996b).

9. To check the validity of this response, we asked a sample of small business owners what they thought of different reasons why people go into business. Three-fourths (74%) of this entrepreneurial group strongly agreed with the statement that the reason people go into business was "to be their own boss."

10. The lower rating that youth gave to earning lots of money relative to being your own boss as the reason for starting a business may

seem at odds with the greater importance that youth (regardless of their entrepreneurial inclinations) attached to a monetary reason when asked about the possible reasons why other people start a business in another question. These responses were not contradictory. Youth thought that earning lots of money was less important as a motivating reason when they wanted to start a business. They thought it was more important as a motivating reason when others wanted to start a business. This misperception about the motivation of others compared with your own motivation if you were put into that situation suggests an area where more education would be beneficial.

11.   In our subgroup analysis of youth, we found few significant differences in the reasons stated for wanting to start a business among females and males, or among whites, blacks and Hispanics. Females who were interested in starting a business were only somewhat more likely than males who were interested in starting a business to think the reason for doing so was "to be my own boss" (43% versus 40%). Females were also somewhat less likely than males to think that the reason was "to earn lots of money" (18% versus 24%). Blacks were less likely than whites (39% versus 44%) to think that it was "to be my own boss" and more likely to think that it was "to help the community or provide jobs" (12% versus 7%). Hispanics were significantly less likely than other youth to think that the motivation for entrepreneurship was "to be my own boss" (31%) but significantly more likely to think that it was "to build something for the family" (11% versus 5%).

12.   We also investigated the subgroup difference. The results showed that there were minimal differences in the reasons given for not starting a business among females and males, or among blacks, whites and Hispanics. A few differences, however, among blacks, whites and Hispanics are worth noting, despite the small samples on which the results are based. Blacks were equally likely to cite a lack of money or financial capital (22%), a lack of energy, time, skills or ideas (22%), or to prefer their current situation (22%). Whites were more likely to cite energy, time, skills or ideas (27%) or to prefer their current situation (19%). Hispanics were more likely to cite problems with managing a business (28%) or business risk (21%) as reasons for not wanting to start a business.

13. Elementary teachers were significantly more likely than senior high teachers to cite a lack of energy, time, skills or ideas as reasons for not starting a business (30% versus 21%). Elementary teachers were significantly less likely than senior high teachers to cite age as a reason for not starting a business (10% versus 22%). Business educators at the middle school/junior high level thought more about the problems of managing a business than did social studies teachers (18% versus 9%).

LOOKING GOOD:
Views of Small Business

If you let people choose between being a small business owner or a manager in a large corporation, how do you think they would reply?

Big Companies, Big Things

A strong case could be made that most would overwhelmingly

choose the latter. After all, on the surface there appears to be more status in saying you work for a large corporation, such as Ford, IBM or Monsanto, as opposed to saying you're the owner of Bender's Pest Control, the Patio Cafe or Bunker Hill Brick.

A position in a large corporation may also convey the feeling that you are performing a more important role in the economy, because "big companies do big things." For example, you may believe that you are responsible for making cars, paper, or steel, or delivering important services related to banking, insurance and travel.

Finally, with a corporate position often come the trappings of office—income, benefits and executive offices—along with power and control over many employees.

The Never-Ending Story

Contrast these attributes with those typically associated with a small business owner. The owner probably has no staff assistants. His or her office may be in a low-rise building such as a retail establishment, small office complex or a factory—instead of a large, impressive edifice. Further, the small business owner probably dresses and acts more like the employees or customers.

There are fewer status benefits or perks of the office for being the owner of a small business, because the owner recognizes that spending money on such benefits reduces the firm's profits—so he or she would rather plow the money back into the business.

Then there are all of the headaches with being a small business owner: being responsible at all times for the business and never getting completely away from the burden of this responsibility. The owner must be willing to assume not only the financial risk but all the stress that accompanies managing a small business and keeping it growing. Given these perceived differences in status, along with the full-time demands and stresses, why would anyone want to be a small business owner?

Ownership Versus Management

We decided to find out what youth thought about the choice of being a manager in a large corporation versus being a small business owner. Our initial expectation was that they would overwhelmingly prefer the corporate position given the above contrasts. Even though the contrasts may be based more on stereotypes than reality, many people seem to perceive that a corporate position is more powerful, of higher status and better-paying.

What the survey revealed was pleasantly surprising. Many youth were not overwhelmed by the idea of a corporate job and could clearly appreciate the positive qualities of small-business ownership. When given a choice between being a small-business owner or a manager in a large corporation, well over half would rather be an owner. These results are a further indication of the positive view that many youth had toward entrepreneurship.

TABLE 3.1:   Small-Business Owner or Manager in Large Corporation

Response	Youth	General Public	Teachers	Business Owners
	(n=1,008)	(600)	(1,609)	(204)
	%	%	%	%
A small business owner	56	73	76	89
A manager in a large corporation	43	23	20	9
Both	0	0	0	0
Neither	0	3	3	0
Don't know	1	2	0	2

Other Voices, Other Views. Similar results hold for the general public but are even more dramatic. If given a choice, about three-fourths of the general public would choose small-business ownership over being a manager in a large corporation. Teachers responded in much the same way: about three-fourths of them would rather be small-business owners if they had to choose between the two occupations. The great majority of the general public and teachers were evidently not swayed by the power and prestige of working as a manager for a large corporation. Conversely, they did seem to recognize and appreciate the benefits of small-business ownership.

The same question was posed to small-business owners to find out if they were satisfied with their job or career decision. Obviously, the fact that they had already chosen to own a small business suggests that many of them are satisfied with that choice—but we did not know to what extent it was the prevailing attitude.

The survey results were impressive, showing that the very great majority of small-business owners were satisfied with their choice. Few occupations exist wherein nine in 10 people are satisfied with their job choice! Small-business owners apparently like what they are doing, and almost all find working as a manager for a large corporation to be a much less appealing alternative.[1]

Gender, Race, Ethnicity. Our investigation found some interesting results when we looked at the responses of youth by gender. Female youth were significantly more interested in becoming small-business owners than were male youth (60% versus 53%). What this result suggests is that when females think about their entry into the business world, a larger majority are likely to think of themselves as small-business owners rather than corporate managers. One of the reasons we are seeing more women-owned businesses in the economy may be that women are acting on this youthful preference to work for themselves rather than for someone else, and in the process maintain more control over their lives.

The breakdowns in responses by race and ethnicity tell a vastly different story. A significantly smaller percentage of blacks than whites (44% versus 61%) preferred small-business ownership over corporate management. Hispanics were about evenly split between their enthusiasm for small-business ownership (48%) or a corporate management position (51%).

Although black youth are more interested in starting a business than are white youth (see Chapter 2), if given a choice, many would nevertheless prefer a corporate management position.

This conflicting response may arise from a number of factors. For instance, black youth may feel less prepared or confident in acting on their entrepreneurial interest and thus select the more risk-averse position of working for someone else. Black youth may also have less direct access to role models for entrepreneurship, an issue which will be explored later in this chapter. We can only speculate about the possible reasons, but they do suggest an area where more education about entrepreneurship would be of value for encouraging black youth to explore a wider array of business and employment options.

David Versus Goliath

We did some further probing to find out what youth and adults thought about American small business with respect to four attributes: (1) providing services that meet customers' needs; (2) paying workers for what they accomplish; (3) producing quality products at reasonable prices; and (4) providing jobs. Our strategy was to ask the groups to compare American small businesses with large corporations on these attributes and tell us whether they thought most small businesses were better, worse or about the same.

On any question that offers respondents three options from which to choose, a split response is likely to be given. Nevertheless, what remains of interest is the direction in which most people are leaning. Do they favor the better or worse side, or simply see little difference between small businesses and large corporations on these four attributes?

Providing Needed Services. As might be expected, the most positive response came on the issue of providing services that meet customers' needs. This is probably due to the tendency of small businesses to seek competitive advantage through personal service. Among youth, more than five in 10 thought small businesses were better at providing these services than large corporations, while only one in 10 thought they were worse.[2] The general public and teachers, however, were significantly more enthusiastic: some two-thirds stated that small businesses were better than large corporations at providing services to meet customers' needs.[3] The most positive perspective came from small-business owners, most of whom thought small businesses were better than large corporations in offering services that meet customers' needs.[4]

TABLE 3.2: Small Businesses Compared to Large Corporations

Response	Youth (n=1,008)	General Public (600)	Teachers (1,609)	Business Owners (204)
	%	%	%	%
A. Producing quality products at reasonable prices				
Better	43	44	29	52
Worse	17	18	28	15
About same	39	34	42	29
Don't know	1	4	1	3
B. Providing services that meet customers' needs				
Better	54	66	66	86
Worse	10	7	9	4
About same	34	24	25	9
Don't know	1	3	1	0
C. Paying workers for what they accomplish				
Better	44	32	22	45
Worse	16	31	43	24
About same	37	31	33	30
Don't know	2	6	3	1
D. Providing jobs				
Better	27	31	24	50
Worse	40	32	49	27
About same	32	31	25	22
Don't know	1	6	2	2

Producing Quality. Perspectives were more mixed on whether small businesses were better at producing quality products at reasonable prices. Youth were fairly positive in their views, with more than four in 10 opining that small businesses were better, compared to fewer than two in 10 who thought they were worse. This response was essentially equivalent to that of the general public, where more than four in 10 also thought small business was better at producing quality products at reasonable prices. Also holding a positive view were small-business owners. In contrast to the services issue, however, only about five in 10 thought small businesses were better at providing quality products at reasonable prices.

The most negative group on the quality and price issue was teachers. About an equal percentage of teachers said small businesses were better as said they were worse. The plurality of teachers, however, thought they were about the same, with about four in 10 selecting this option. In other words, when the topic was producing quality products, teachers appeared to be more skeptical about the advantages of small businesses. While it is unclear how this perception might affect the teaching of entrepreneurship or the quality of information supplied about small business, the response caught our attention.

Checking on Pay. We became more concerned when we compared the thinking of teachers with other groups on the issue of whether small businesses were better, worse or about the same at paying workers for what they accomplish. Many American youth held a positive view and thought that small businesses were better at paying workers for what they accomplish, while only a minority thought they were worse. In fact, the position of youth was very similar to small-business owners. The general public was more ambivalent on the question. About an equal percentage selected each of the three ratings.

In contrast to these responses, consider the reaction of teachers. Only about two in 10 thought small businesses were better at paying workers for what they accomplish, whereas almost twice as many thought they were worse. After seeing this response, we were again wondering why teachers' views of small business were so out of line with the others and so negative toward small business.

Providing Jobs. Our suspicions that teachers held a more negative view of small business than other groups was confirmed when we asked them to evaluate small businesses in terms of providing jobs. On this issue, teachers had the most negative perspective. Less than a quarter of teachers were of the opinion that small businesses were better than large corporations at providing jobs, but about half thought small businesses were worse.[5]

The views of youth were similar to teachers, albeit not as negative. More than a quarter of youth thought small businesses were better at providing jobs, while four in 10 held the opposite opinion. Just as they had on the pay issue, the general public held a split opinion on jobs provided. About three in 10 of the general public said small businesses were either better, worse or about the same as large corporations. As might be expected, small-business owners were the most positive in their assessment of this issue. Fully five in 10 thought small businesses were better at providing jobs, while only about a quarter thought they were worse.

These results, especially from teachers and youth, show that many people misunderstand the important contribution of small business to jobs creation in the national economy. Small businesses account for over half of the jobs in the economy and are also responsible for creating the most net new jobs (jobs added minus jobs lost).[6] Furthermore, small businesses are often the first entry point into the labor force for youth and younger adults.

We did not really expect youth to know about the important role small businesses play in providing jobs in the U.S. economy, but we did expect teachers to be somewhat more informed on the issue and their perceptions to be more positive. Teachers' views on the job, pay and quality aspects of small-business issues foster speculation about how small businesses are portrayed in the classroom and how the perceptions of teachers affect youth

39

interest in entrepreneurship. We will address this subject in the next chapter, when we look at knowledge of entrepreneurship, and in a later chapter on entrepreneurship education.

Gender, Race, Ethnicity. There were no significant differences between females and males when their views of small businesses and large corporations were compared. Females were slightly less likely than males to think small businesses were better than large corporations in providing quality products (40% versus 46%) or in paying workers (41% versus 47%). Equal percentages thought that small businesses were better in offering quality products at reasonable prices (54%). The major topic on which small businesses were viewed as worse by females and males was in providing jobs: 38% of females and 42% of males thought small businesses were worse (an insignificant disparity).

Compared with whites, blacks held a less favorable view of the features of small business. This response is consistent with that found in the owner-versus-manager question. A significantly smaller percentage of blacks than whites thought small businesses were better at providing services (47% versus 57%) or at paying workers for what they accomplish (36% versus 46%). Blacks were divided into about thirds on the issue of whether small businesses were better (31%), worse (33%) or about the same (35%) as large corporations in providing jobs. Whites were more likely to think they were worse (43%) than better (26%) or about the same (30%).

A plurality of Hispanics (43%) thought that small businesses were better at producing quality products at reasonable prices. A significantly smaller percentage of Hispanics than other youth (45% versus 56%) considered small businesses better at providing services. A smaller percentage of Hispanics than other youth (38% versus 45%) thought small businesses were better at paying workers. Hispanics and other youth showed little difference on the issue of providing jobs. Most Hispanics thought small businesses were worse (39%), not better (25%), than large corporations.

Reporting on Role Models

We thought it was also important to find out if youth knew or had any personal contact with a small-business owner who could offer insight into how small business worked or serve as a role model. In fact, studies of entrepreneurship have reported that role models have a critical influence on entrepreneurial aspirations and achievement. The more likely people are to know someone who owned a business, the more likely they might be interested in starting a business because they have a role model to follow.[7]

TABLE 3.3: Know a Person Who Runs a Small Business

Response	Youth (n=1,008)	General Public (600)
	%	%
Yes	57	77
No	43	23

We asked youth this question: *Do you personally know a person who runs a small business?* The response was about split. Somewhat more than half said they did, and somewhat fewer than half did not. What these responses indicate is that many youth lack personal exposure to small business or do not know a role model who might stimulate their interest in entrepreneurship. For these students, any insights about small business and entrepreneurship will most likely have to come from the instruction they receive in school. By contrast, more than three-fourths of the general public knew someone who ran a small business.

41

(Given their higher average age and broader work experience, the general public could be expected to have this higher level of contact with small business.)

We also looked at the differences in the results by gender, race and ethnicity. There was no significant difference in the response of males and females as to whether they knew someone who ran a small business.

There was, however, a significant and sizable difference by race and ethnicity. More than six in 10 (62%) of the white youth reported they knew someone who ran a small business, whereas fewer than five in 10 (47%) black youth or Hispanic youth (48%) said they knew someone who ran a small business. The results suggest that black and Hispanic youth are likely to face a disadvantage if they want to start a business because they have less access to entrepreneurs as role models. The results also suggest that black and Hispanic youth are more likely to benefit from an entrepreneurial education or experiences which afford more exposure to such role models.

Award-Winning Roles. We decided to do some further probing of our initial question with one that asked youth who said they knew someone who ran a small business to describe the relationship with that person: was it a parent, a relative, a friend, a neighbor or someone else? The predominant responses, given by almost two-thirds, were either "a friend" or "a relative."

These responses are consistent with those found among the general public. Also, few youth, or the general public for that matter, identified their boss or employer as a small-business owner. A quarter of youth who said they knew someone who ran a small business said it was their parents.[8]

Further analysis based on race proved to be insightful. We found that black youth were significantly less likely than white youth to cite a parent (13% versus 26%) and significantly more likely to identify a relative (40% versus 19%) as someone they knew who ran a small business. (The responses of Hispanic youth were quite similar to those of whites.)

TABLE 3.4: Relationship to Person Who Runs a Small Business

Response	Youth (n=579)*	General Public (460)*
	%	%
Friend	43	47
Relative	21	20
Boss/Employer	2	8
Parent	25	7
Myself	0	7
Neighbor	6	3
Someone else	2	7

Only those who knew a person who ran a small business.

The difference between black and white youth is important because studies have shown the more personal his or her relationship with a small-business owner, the more likely a person is to start a business. The closer personal relationship to a parent, as opposed to a relative or friend, would appear to be more effective as a role model in influencing the entrepreneurial aspirations of youth, and on this issue blacks may be at a disadvantage relative to whites. Again, an effective education in entrepreneurship may be needed to overcome this role-model gap.

Challenging Perceptions

When people start a small business, they expect there to be challenges in making it successful. These challenges may involve competing with other businesses; developing sales; obtaining loans and financing; or handling government regulation and red tape. What we wanted to find out from youth was which of the

challenges they thought would prove to be more difficult than initially expected by people who start a new business. As a reality check, the same question was asked of the general public and of small-business owners. The contrast revealed several major misperceptions on the part of youth.

TABLE 3.5: Challenges That Prove More Difficult Than Expected in Starting a New Business

Response	Youth	General Public	Business Owners
	(n=1,008)	(600)	(204)
	%	%	%
Competing with other businesses	79	78	65
Obtaining loans and financing	71	75	79
Developing sales	74	76	65
Controlling costs	72	77	73
Handling government regulation and red tape	56	75	87

American youth thought there were many challenges to starting a business that would prove to be more difficult than initially anticipated. Almost eight in 10 cited competing with other businesses, while about seven in 10 cited developing sales, controlling costs, and obtaining loans and financing. The responses of the general public to the challenges were essentially the same as youth. These results were not surprising, because competitive or financial problems of business are widely reported in the news media.

Small-business owners saw the business world from a different perspective—one based on their actual experience. They did agree with youth and the general public that controlling costs and obtaining loans and financing proved to be more difficult challenges than they had expected. They were less likely, however, to agree that competing with other businesses or developing sales were harder than expected.

The most unexpected challenge, according to nearly nine in 10 small-business owners, was handling government regulation and red tape. This percentage was far higher than the response given for any other of the other challenges considered.

The only other group to recognize this problem was the general public, three-quarters of whom agreed that government regulation and red tape would prove to be more difficult than initially expected when starting a business. By contrast, fewer than six in 10 youth thought this to be the case.[10]

If this lack of recognition is not to become a factor limiting entrepreneurial success, young people need to be made more aware of it through education or other means. The failure to see the government-regulation problem as more difficult than expected also reflects a lack of entrepreneurial knowledge among youth—a topic we explore in the next chapter.

1. We do not have comparative data for corporate managers, but
    some anecdotal evidence suggests a degree of dissatisfaction
    with that job choice. When corporations offer job buyouts,
    many want to use the funds to start their own business. For further
    discussion of making the transition from executive to entrepre-
    neur, see Zoghlin (1991).

2. This response is consistent with that from an open-ended question
    that asked, "What do you like most about American small busi-
    ness?" Almost six in 10 (58%) youth thought of a positive feature
    of small business that they liked. The customer and personal ser-
    vice dimension of small business was the most appreciated, cited
    by about a quarter (23%). Fewer mentioned jobs and employee
    relations (15%), economic opportunity and freedom (7%) or
    competition and competitiveness (6%). Many youth (42%), how-
    ever, gave a "don't know" (38%) or a "nothing" (4%) response.
    One reason for the "don't know" or "nothing" responses may be
    the difficulty of replying to this open-ended question. These
    responses also suggest that a large percentage of youth lack knowl-
    edge about small business, an explanation that is supported by
    their answers to other survey questions in Chapter 4.

3. When the general public was asked what they liked most about
    small business in an open-ended question, about three-fourths
    (74%) identified a positive feature. The most noted feature,
    cited by one-third (33%), was the customer and personal service
    offered by small business. Other features cited, by much smaller
    percentages, were economic opportunity and freedom (13%),
    jobs and employee relations (10%), and competition and com-
    petitiveness (8%); other responses totalled 10%. Only a quarter
    of the general public gave a "don't know" (19%) or a "nothing"
    (6%) response.

4. Nine in 10 (88%) of small-business owners stated a feature of
    small business that they liked in an open-ended question. The
    largest percentage (50%) thought the most appealing feature of
    small business was the economic opportunity and freedom it
    gave the people who ran the business. The reason why their per-
    spective differs from the general public, and from some youth, is
    that in this open-ended question small-business owners probably
    thought about small businesses as producers, and therefore gave
    economic freedom and opportunity more importance. The general
    public and high school students looked at small businesses in

their roles as consumers, and thus gave more emphasis to the customer and personal service aspects of small business.

5.   There were few significant differences among teachers by the level of schooling or subject taught. Elementary teachers were less likely than middle school/junior high or senior high teachers to think that small businesses were better than large corporations at providing jobs (16% versus 25% or 32%). Senior high teachers were significantly more likely to recognize that small businesses were better at providing jobs (32%), and significantly less likely to say small business was worse at providing jobs than other teachers (38% versus 55% and 51%).

    Among elementary teachers, upper grade or intermediate teachers were significantly more likely than lower grade or primary teachers to think that small business was about the same at providing services (33% versus 21%), although the majority of teachers in both groups had a positive perspective of this attribute of small business. Among senior high teachers, business educators were significantly less likely than teachers of other subjects to think that small business was better at paying workers (17% versus 24%). Other teachers were significantly more likely than business education or social studies teachers (46% versus 35% or 33%) to think that small businesses were worse at providing jobs.

6.   See Dennis (1993, pp. 16-17).

7.   For a discussion of role models and entrepreneurship, see Green and Pryde (1990). One national survey of young adults found a strong relationship between having an entrepreneurial role model in the form of a parent, family member or friend and expecting to own a business in the future (see Development Associates, 1993).

8.   This percentage seemed too high to us, but we had no way of verifying it. We think the inflated percentage probably reflects both youth's lack of knowledge about small business and their misperception about the occupation or employment of their parents.

9.   See Development Associates (1993), and Green and Pryde (1990).

10.   There were few differences in the perceptions of females and males, blacks and whites, or Hispanics about challenges that

prove to be more difficult than initially anticipated for entrepreneurs. A significantly greater percentage of females than males believed that developing sales (77% versus 71%), or controlling costs (75% versus 69%), would prove to be more difficult than initially expected for someone starting a business. Hispanics thought that developing sales (82%) would prove to be more difficult than anticipated.

GETTING BACK TO BASICS:
Knowledge of Entrepreneurship

Young people who display an interest in starting a business face a more difficult path if they lack the basic knowledge that prepares them for the challenges they may face as an entrepreneur, that helps them consider opportunities and see solutions to business problems, and gives them the ability to understand how business and a market economy work—as well as the entrepreneur's role in both. That is why a major objective of our study was to find out what youth knew about entrepreneurship and related concepts. We also wanted this information to help us develop insights about the entrepreneurship education provided by the schools and identify areas for improvement.

Multiple Choice, Singular Goal

Time constraints and the limits of interviewing precluded giving youth an extensive paper-and-pencil test of their knowledge. Instead, we believed a short test would provide the baseline information and insights we sought. To this end, we prepared a test of eight multiple-choice questions covering a range of topics related to entrepreneurship, small business and economics. We considered them to be a representative sample of the knowledge questions that could have been asked.[1]

Precautions were taken to ensure the questions would provide useful information. Questions were written to be easily understood by youth and then field tested to evaluate likely responses before involving the national sample. We even had the questions reviewed for content accuracy by a national panel of 10 experts in entrepreneurship, small business and economics. Survey experts at Gallup also checked the wording of the questions to eliminate potential bias or misleading terms. In short, we established a high level of confidence that we were using a valid and reliable set of questions to measure basic knowledge of entrepreneurship.[2]

The questions also were composed with the objective of administering them to the three other groups surveyed, in addition to youth. The objective was to see how these groups performed relative to youth, with the working hypothesis being that these other groups would all do better because they have more work experience or education. We also anticipated there would be a predictable rank order in the overall scores on the eight items, based on the degree of business experience and education. In our expected ranking, small-business owners would have the highest overall scores, followed by teachers, the general public and youth.

Making the Grade

One point should be noted to put the test results into perspective: we did not expect any group to answer correctly all the test items, even small-business owners. On most tests, there will be some items that are easy to answer and others that prove to be more difficult and challenging. The primary reason for this is that ability, education and business experience differ among individuals, even within the same group. Some individuals may know more about the topics tested, while others know less.

The respondents also were asked the questions "cold" and given no preparation or review (as commonly would occur in a course). In addition, there can be a degree of measurement error in questions that tends to reduce overall scores. Given all of this, we thought an average score of 70 percent correct or better would indicate reasonable mastery of the material. So, that percentage was established as a cutoff for the purposes of analysis. We expected to see scores at least this high among the small-business owners but not among the other groups.[3]

In the sections that follow, we first discuss the overall scores to examine what they tell us about entrepreneurship knowledge among youth. We will then turn to the item results to identify questions on which students did relatively better or worse.

Probing the Gaps

The rank order for overall scores among the groups turned out as expected. Youth had a mean score of 42 percent correct, which was the lowest of all the groups. These results indicate that there were substantial gaps in their knowledge of entrepreneurship and related topics in business and economics.[4]

The obvious follow-up question was, "Why don't students know more?" Two explanations seemed most plausible.

First, as discussed in the previous chapter, most youth have limited exposure to business owners. Many do not know someone who operates a business—and even when they do, the person may not be someone with whom they have a close relationship.

Second, we believe business and economic education in the schools may be inadequate or incomplete at times. Too few students appear to receive much of an education about entrepreneurship through business education and economics courses, a factor which we think directly affects youth's knowledge and understanding of these subjects. Supporting evidence on this latter point is found in Chapter 7.

TABLE 4.1: Percentage of Correct Responses to Entrepreneurial-Knowledge Questions

	Youth	General Public	Teachers	Business Owners
	(n=1,008)	(600)	(1,609)	(204)
	%	%	%	%
1. Description of entrepreneur	73	78	89	89
2. Small business and job creation	25	46	54	65
3. Double taxation of corporations	39	27	27	50
4. Typical way to raise capital	12	21	19	51
5. Cash flow	46	54	72	90
6. Example of franchise	62	80	97	96
7. Supply and demand	51	59	86	86
8. Purpose of profits	25	33	50	62
Mean % correct	**42**	**50**	**62**	**74**

Does Older Mean Wiser? How did the other groups do? The general public scored only slightly better than youth, getting 50 percent correct. We did not expect this group to score much higher than youth, simply because many of them had only a limited business education in high school or college. Although the greater work experience and education of the general public may have helped their scores relative to youth, the results suggest it may not have been all that much help.

Teachers scored significantly higher than the general public and could correctly answer an average of 62 percent of the items. Further analysis provided some interesting contrasts. The average percent correct for elementary teachers (56%) was significantly lower than that for senior high school teachers (66%). The likely reason for this difference was that elementary teachers took few courses in entrepreneurship or economics compared with secondary teachers.[5] At the secondary level, one would expect business-education teachers to have the highest scores, but their average scores (69%) were not significantly greater than those for social studies teachers (66%). Business-educator scores were, however, significantly higher than the scores of math, science or language arts teachers (62%).

As anticipated, small-business owners scored the highest on our test, with 74 percent correct. Their scores were not 100 percent correct, but we did not expect this outcome due to the nature of testing and the effects of individual differences on test scores that were previously discussed. The score of 74 percent correct, however, was clearly above the cutoff score that was set to indicate mastery of the material. This score provides some evidence to support the validity of the test, as one would expect those who know more to score higher than those who know less. This pattern is evident across all groups surveyed.

We now turn to the responses the groups gave for each question. The following analysis rank orders correct responses to eight questions on those topics on which youth scored high, average and low. These item results provide further insights about knowledge of entrepreneurship.

More Knowledge, More Insights

Youth scored the highest on two definition questions, one on the entrepreneur and the other on franchise.

Identifying Entrepreneurs. The first question asked the respondent to identify a simple definition of an entrepreneur—a person who owns a small business—to determine if youth had a good idea of what the term meant.[6] We expected students to do well on this question, expectations which were confirmed when more than seven in 10 selected the correct answer. About a quarter, however, thought an entrepreneur was either a manager of a large corporation, a government official running a regulatory agency, or did not know. Especially disconcerting was the fact that one in 10 youth thought an entrepreneur was a government official running a regulatory agency.

The general public scored somewhat better than youth on this question, with almost eight in 10 identifying the correct description. We also expected a high percentage correct from both teachers and small-business owners, and found exactly that. About nine in 10 of each of these two groups gave the correct response.

Building Franchises. Another question on which students did well involved identifying a franchise. The reason we asked this question was because franchising has become one of the most common ways for an entrepreneur to go into business.[7]

To check their understanding, we asked them to select an example of a franchise business from a set of possible choices. About six in 10 youth selected a correct example of a franchise: a McDonald's restaurant. These encouraging results were tempered, however, by the fact that almost four in 10 thought a franchise was the IBM corporation or a General Motors-Oldsmobile plant.[8]

Eight in 10 of the general public selected the correct answer to the franchise question, which was a significantly higher percentage than youth (we suspect the job or business experience of this group accounts for their greater knowledge). Teachers and small-business owners also achieved their highest scores on this question. In fact, nearly all of the surveyed samples selected the correct answer. Given the relative simplicity of the question, though, any other result would have been worrisome.

TABLE 4.2: Entrepreneurial-Knowledge Questions

Item and Response	Youth	General Public	Teachers	Business Owners
	(n=1,008)	(600)	(1,609)	(204)
	%	%	%	%
1. Which of the following best describes an entrepreneur?				
*A person who owns a small business	73	78	89	89
A manager of a large corporation	14	8	5	5
A government official running a regulatory agency	9	6	2	1
Don't know/Other	4	7	4	4
2. Which one of these businesses is the best example of a franchise?				
*A McDonald's restaurant	62	80	97	96
A General Motors-Oldsmobile plant	15	10	1	1
The IBM corporation	22	7	1	2
Don't know/Other	2	3	1	1
3. To the best of your knowledge, the prices of most products in a competitive market, like the United States, are determined by the:				
*Supply and demand for products	51	59	86	86
Consumer Price Index	20	20	7	7
Local, state or federal government	20	9	1	1
Monetary policy of the Federal Reserve	4	2	2	2
Don't know/Other	5	10	3	3

Continued on next page

	Youth	General Public	Teachers	Business Owners
4. Which factor is most important for business survival?				
*The company's cash flow	46	54	72	90
The value of the company's common stock	22	15	13	2
Having a low depreciation rate	15	12	6	2
Having a board of directors	13	10	3	1
Don't know/Other	3	9	5	3
5. For which type of business organization is the owner or are the owners subject to DOUBLE taxation by the federal government?				
*Corporations	39	27	27	50
Partnerships	25	19	15	12
Sole proprietorships	7	11	24	16
Cooperatives	19	9	6	3
Don't know/Other	10	32	29	18
6. Over the past 10 years, which of the following groups has created the most new jobs in the economy?				
*Small business	25	46	54	58
Large businesses	47	26	31	23
The federal government	25	20	10	13
Don't know/Other	3	7	6	4
7. Which of the following do you think is the basic purpose of profits in our market economy?				
*Reward businesses for producing what consumers want	25	33	50	62
Pay for the wages and salaries of workers	50	40	28	28
Transfer income to the wealthy	21	19	16	5
Don't know/Other	2	7	2	4
8. Considering the methods of raising capital to start a new business, which of the following is the most typical?				
*Using personal money or borrowing from friends or relatives	12	21	19	51
Borrowing money from a bank	60	55	56	38
Borrowing money from the government	17	11	8	2
Issuing company stock or bonds to the general public	9	6	7	3
Don't know/Other	2	6	10	5

*Correct Response

Doing the Splits

Students were approximately half right and half wrong on two items, one related to economics and the other to business.

Supply and Demand. Because knowledge of some economics also serves as an underpinning for entrepreneurship, we included a few questions on the survey which probed for some economic understanding about how a market economy works. One question involved identifying how the prices of most products are determined in a market economy.

Those familiar with economics would know that prices are determined in a competitive market by the supply of and demand for products. Thus, it is generally competition, and not some institutional or government mechanism, which allocates resources and establishes prices.

Just five in 10 knew the prices of most products in a market economy like the United States were determined by the forces of supply and demand. Two in 10 believed the prices of most products were determined by the consumer price index (which is simply a measure of inflation). Another two in 10 thought the prices were determined by government. A few even thought prices were set by the monetary policy of the Federal Reserve.[9]

The results from the general public were not much better. Only about six in 10 recognized that most prices are determined by supply and demand.

Clearly, these results suggest a need for some remedial education on this issue for youth and the general public. This conclusion was only reinforced by our finding that most of the general public and youth want government intervention to control the prices of products, an issue we'll discuss in the next chapter. By contrast, the great majority of teachers and small-business owners—almost nine in 10—appear to understand and appreciate the important role the interaction of supply and demand plays in the economy.[10]

Cash Flow. For a new business to survive, one of the most critical factors is whether it has the cash flow to meet its financial obligations. We asked a question that would assess this vital understanding.

What we found was that about half of youth recognized the importance of cash flow. The other half incorrectly believed that business survival was dependent on something else that was not essential: the value of the company's stock. The reason this answer is incorrect is because stock prices can rise and fall at any time, and not all firms issue stock. The firm's depreciation rate is also an incorrect answer, because it is just a cost factor. A board of directors is certainly not essential for business survival—and is not even a requirement for sole proprietorships and partnerships.

Although many youth may be interested in starting a business, many also fail to recognize the importance of adequate cash flow and thus are ill-prepared to run one.

The responses of the adult groups show some interesting differences. The general public gave answers that closely matched those of youth, probably because most of them have no experience in running a business. Teachers showed a higher level of understanding, but this was expected because many teachers have taken some business courses.

On this question, however, there is a substantial gap between the thinking of teachers and small-business owners. Most teachers—about seven in 10—saw the importance of cash flow.[11] Nine in 10 small-business owners surveyed also recognized this vital need. On this question business experience counts, because it is impossible to stay in business without meeting cash obligations such as supplier invoices, rent and payroll.

Mistakes and Misunderstandings

We also asked youth questions related to taxation, jobs creation, profits and finance, all important topics for someone considering starting a business. The great majority did not know the correct answers.

Taxing Knowledge. The owners of corporations are subject to double taxation by the federal government, because income paid out in the form of dividends is taxed first as part of corporate profits and second as part of the personal income of owners or stockholders. This disadvantage of the corporate structure is one of several reasons why many entrepreneurs often start their business as sole proprietorships.[12]

Fewer than four in 10 youth knew the corporate structure for a business was subject to this extra financial liability. This lack of understanding was evident among the general public and teachers as well—surprisingly—even more so than for youth. Most of the general public may well have guessed the answer, because only about a quarter selected the correct answer from the four choices given.

Even teachers stumbled on this question; only a quarter of this group were able to supply the correct answer. Teacher responses, however, varied significantly based on the grade level or subject taught. Secondary teachers were somewhat more knowledgeable (31%) than elementary teachers (23%), but even the score among secondary teachers was below the correct percentage for youth. Business educators at the middle school/junior high level scored about the same as youth (35%), while business educators in senior high scored slightly higher (46%). These results suggest a topic for which some supplementary education for all teachers is needed.

The most knowledgeable group was small-business owners. Half of them supplied the correct answer, a level which nonetheless indicates the question was a challenging one. Although we expected this correct percentage to be higher, there may be reasons why it was not. We suspect that a number of small-business owners did not know the answer because the business structure under which many small businesses operate is either a sole proprietorship or partnership. Many owners may simply have had less experience, or less need to know, about this disadvantage for the corporate structure because they do not use it.[13]

Staying on Top of the Jobs. Small business has been largely responsible for creating the most new jobs in the economy. Although during any year jobs are created and lost in the economy, by some estimates small business accounted for about two-thirds of the net new jobs created by the economy in recent decades. In addition, those starting new businesses, and not just those expanding existing businesses, accounted for about half of all these net new jobs. Small business is clearly a major contributor to employment growth in the economy, which occurs throughout the ups and downs of the business cycle.[14]

We wanted to find out to what extent youth and adults were aware of the important role that small business and entrepreneurship play in adding jobs. We did not expect this awareness to be particularly high among youth, due to the substantial attention given in the media and by advertisers to large firms such as General Motors, Nike or Sears.

The survey showed that just a quarter of youth were aware of the contribution that small business makes to jobs creation. Almost half were more likely to give the credit for jobs creation to large businesses, and a quarter even thought most new jobs came from the federal government!

This misperception about how the economy works may explain why youth held a negative view when asked whether small business was better or worse than large business in creating jobs (see Table 3.2). This confusion is important to correct, because most youth need to understand which sector of the economy will be the most likely source of their first job and subsequent employment.

On the jobs issue, adult groups showed significantly better knowledge. We suspect that work experience, rather than knowledge about the macro economy, may be the most important factor explaining these higher scores. Somewhat less than half of the general public gave a correct answer, compared to somewhat more than half of teachers. The teacher responses, however, varied by grade level taught. Elementary teachers were significantly less aware (42%) than were secondary teachers (60%) about the important role of small business in jobs creation.[15]

Almost six in 10 business owners recognized the contribution small business makes to jobs creation in the economy. A reason this percentage was not even higher may be that many small-business owners see only their individual contribution to employment and not the aggregate contribution made by small business. In other words, they were looking at the question from a "micro" perspective as we sought an answer from a "macro" perspective.

A Defining Moment for Profits. One of the most misunderstood terms in business and economics is the term "profit." We wanted to include a question about profit on the test because understanding it is a foundation for understanding how markets work. Although many questions could be asked, we decided to find out what youth knew about its basic purpose in a market economy. In this case, profit serves as a reward for entrepreneurs who identify business opportunities and assume the risk to produce those products consumers want.[16]

What did youth think was the purpose of profit? Half thought it was to pay for the wages and salaries of workers. Almost another quarter thought the purpose was to transfer income to the wealthy. Thus, about three-quarters of youth saw profit as some mechanism for redistribution to serve either workers or the wealthy. Only a quarter saw profit as a reward for assuming the risk of producing what the consumer wants.

Youth were not alone in their misunderstandings. Only a third of the general public knew the purpose of profits in a market economy. This result, combined with those from the previous question on supply and demand, indicates that both youth and the general public lack a sound understanding about how a market economy works. This deficiency may have something to do with their business and economic education, and we will address that possibility in Chapter 7.

We found that about half of teachers knew what the role of

profits was in a market economy, a result which indicated that teachers knew significantly more about the purpose of profits than youth or the general public. Although we did find differences in teacher scores by the grade level taught (40% elementary and 57% secondary gave a correct response), the low level of knowledge in both groups was still of concern.

As might be expected, the majority of small-business owners displayed the best level of understanding of the profit issue. More than six in 10 identified the correct response. We think the reason the remainder failed to give a correct answer was that they evaluated the question from a micro, rather than a macro, perspective. In this case, these individuals may have been in business as sole proprietorships without employees, and thus mistakenly considered the profits they earned payment for their work.

Playing the Percentages. Before we turn to the final question on the test, let us take a short detour to look at a related knowledge question asked about profit. This knowledge question was open-ended, asking youth to estimate the percentage rate of profit most businesses make as a rate of return on their investment. Over the  past decade, this rate has averaged about 13 percent and ranged from about 10 to 16 percent for most businesses.[17] What we sought from this question was not a single correct percentage, but a reasonable estimate falling within a fairly wide range. We decided to establish 0 to 20 percent as the range because it easily covers the variability in profits and captures most reasonable estimates.

What we found was that youth were most likely to overstate the rate of profits most businesses make as a rate of return on their investment. Less than a quarter gave estimates in the acceptable range. More than half thought it was much greater than it actually was, and about a quarter simply did not know. The median response was 40 percent.

What these results showed was that most youth had little conception about what return on equity business owners could expect to make from a business. Youth were much more likely to overestimate this return, an attitude which could easily lead to grandiose thinking on the part of those wanting to start a business. For the others, the misperception about profits may reflect or lead to negative views of entrepreneurship because it is thought that "entrepreneurs make too much profit."

The adult groups gave better estimates of the rate of return on investment than did youth, with the degree of correctness among the groups moving upward in a predictable fashion. The general public tended to overstate the rate of profit in a way similar to youth, but somewhat less so. Less than a quarter of the general public gave estimates in the correct range, but the median response was 30 percent. Many teachers also overstated the rate of profit as a return on investment. More than four in 10 gave estimates in the correct range, but a similar percentage thought the rate of profit was higher than it actually was.[18] The median response for teachers was 25 percent. Well over half of small-business owners supplied responses in the correct range. The median estimate for this group was 19 percent.

Venturing Into Start-Up Financing. When people start new businesses, they typically obtain most of their start-up funding from the personal money of the owner or from the owner's borrowing money from friends and relatives.[19] The reason most start-ups use owner financing as a principal source of funding is that many lenders are unwilling to make loans. Investors are likewise unwilling to supply venture capital, given the high degree of risk associated with most new ventures. So, if a person wants to start a business, he or she has to finance it with savings, personal resources (e.g., credit cards), or by borrowing money from friends or family. Even if the bank does make a loan, or an investor does provide financial capital for a new business, the lenders will generally want to see personal money put into the business first so the owner bears some of the risk.

We considered this financing question to be the most difficult one on the test, because this aspect of entrepreneurship is not widely known. Consequently, it was not surprising to see low scores from all groups. Six in 10 youth thought financing a new business was simply a matter of borrowing money from a bank, whereas only about one in 10 knew that it typically required personal money or money from family and friends. The general public and teachers also lacked knowledge on this issue, with only about two in 10 supplying a correct answer. The response from teachers was of concern, because if they are to encourage youth to start a business, then they need to be more aware of this predominant source for financing such a venture.[20]

A significantly higher percentage of small-business owners than other groups did know about the importance of personal sources for funding a new business, but still only about five in 10 gave a correct response. We speculate that many small-business owners who bootstrapped their *own* ventures from savings, personal resources and loans from family or friends may have believed their personal experiences were unique and did not reflect the average experiences of other small-business entrepreneurs. It may also be the case that not all the owners we surveyed had started their business, so they might not be aware of what was typical for the start-up entrepreneurs.

Knowing Thyself

Although we tested youth on their knowledge of entrepreneurship and related concepts, we also wondered what these teenagers would say if asked to rate their knowledge or understanding of starting and managing a business. Was it *excellent, good, fair, poor* or *very poor?* We knew there were deficiencies in their entrepreneurial knowledge but wanted to know if they would give an accurate self-assessment of their level of knowledge.

We found a strong correspondence between the knowledge scores and self-rating. Most youth were well aware of their limitations as shown by the low self-ratings. More than four in 10 rated themselves as "poor" or "very poor" in their knowledge and understanding of starting and managing a business. Another four in 10 considered it "fair." Only about two in 10 rated their expertise as "good" or "excellent."[21]

The general public gave an accurate self-assessment of their knowledge and understanding of starting and managing a business. As with youth, four in 10 thought it was "poor" or "very poor." About a third thought it was just "fair." Only a quarter assessed themselves as "excellent" or "good."

TABLE 4.3: **Knowledge and Understanding of Starting and Managing a Business**

Response	Youth (n=1,008)	General Public (600)	Teachers (1,609)
	%	%	%
5 (Excellent)	6	11	3
4 (Good)	12	14	11
3 (Fair)	38	34	36
2 (Poor)	28	19	30
1 (Very Poor)	16	21	19
Don't know	1	0	0

Although teachers got a higher average percent correct than youth or the general public, they too were generally dissatisfied with their knowledge and understanding of starting and managing a business. In fact, almost five in 10 teachers gave themselves a "poor"or "very poor" rating. About a third gave themselves a "fair" rating. About one in six rated themselves "excellent" or "good."

Elementary teachers, who had the lowest knowledge scores of any teacher group, recognized their deficiencies and were highly likely (61%) to rate themselves either "poor" or "very poor" on their knowledge and understanding of entrepreneurship. At the other end of the spectrum were business-education teachers in senior high school, who had the highest average knowledge score. This group evaluated their knowledge and understanding more favorably than any other teacher group (6% excellent and 25% good). This result suggests that at least three in 10 business teachers feel confident in their content background for teaching this subject, but seven in 10 do not.

Knowledge, however, is not the only area of concern here. The opinions people hold shape their views of appropriate policies with respect to the world of business and the role of government—a topic for investigation in the next chapter.

1. In test terminology, it means the questions sample the content domain. Curriculum materials and textbooks on entrepreneurship provide a description of the content domain. For some examples, see Kent (1990), Kourilsky, et al. (1995), Kuratko and Hodgetts (1998), or Lambing and Kuehl (1997). The topics included in this test are found in such materials.

2. Support for the content validity of the survey is based on the extensive review and development work in constructing the survey (Walstad and Kourilsky, 1996). The survey instrument was also a highly reliable measure. This evidence comes from the strong correlation in the percentage responses to survey items when they were administered to two similar national random samples of youth. The correlation between the responses to the same questions given to one national sample (14-18 year olds) and the national sample (14-19 year olds) that we report in this book was .99. When survey items were broken into knowledge and opinion categories, the correlations remained the same— .99 for knowledge and .99 for opinion items.

3. This level for the cutoff score is often used in testing situations that test for the degree of mastery of material. It has been used for math and language arts competency tests for high school students or in written driver's tests for adults. In a pass-fail system of grading, you often need to get at least a "C" grade to get a "pass" in a course. On a 100-point scale, the cutoff for a "C" is usually a 70.

4. The subgroup analysis showed that females and males had about the same mean percent correct (41% versus 42%). Although there was a gap of four to five percentage points in the scores of whites (43%) and blacks (38%) or Hispanics (38%), the differences were not significant.

5. Only 9 percent of elementary teachers reported taking a course in small business or entrepreneurship in college compared with 19 percent of middle school/junior high teachers and 26 percent of senior high teachers. Only 58 percent of elementary teachers said they had taken a course in economics compared with 76 percent of middle school/junior high teachers and 81 percent of senior high teachers.

6. We realize that there are other definitions and descriptions of an entrepreneur that are more complex (see Drucker, 1985;

Kuratko and Hodgetts, 1998; Timmons, 1990; Timmons, 1994). This simple definition was sufficient for our purpose and the age of the youth we surveyed. Given the set of alternatives from which to choose, is it hard to imagine that there would be much support for the incorrect options.

7.   For further discussion of this point, see Lambing and Kuehl (1997, pp. 103-117).

8.   When we examined the data by ethnicity, we found that Hispanics (49%) were significantly less likely than other youth (64%) to give the correct answer. We don't know why that was the case, but the difference did concern us because it indicates that there is some greater misunderstanding about this definition among Hispanic youth.

9.   We were concerned with the results from this question because it was the only knowledge question on which there was a significant difference between the responses of blacks and whites (30% versus 56%). Understanding how a market economy works is an essential part of entrepreneurship, and we wonder about the adequacy of the preparation of black youth for entrepreneurship given this understanding.

10.   A significantly smaller percentage of elementary teachers (81%) recognized this economic relationship compared with secondary teachers (89%). Among secondary teachers, a significantly higher percentage of business-education teachers at the middle/junior high school level gave a correct answer (94%) than social studies teachers (85%).

11.   Senior high teachers were significantly more likely to give a correct response than other teachers (78% versus 68% or 71%). Also, business-education teachers at the middle school/junior high and senior high school levels were correct more often than social studies or other teachers (81% versus 69%; 85% versus 77% and 71%).

12.   See Lambing and Kuehl (1997, pp. 237-238).

13.   The data show that about 75 percent of businesses are proprietorships. For a discussion of the distribution of small businesses across different structures, see Brock and Evans (1986, p. 8) or Dennis (1993, pp. 6-7).

69

14. See Dennis (1993, pp. 16-17) and Reynolds and White (1997, pp. 13-38).

15. Teachers were more correct on this question than youth, but the result only reinforced our suspicions that teachers may hold unwarranted opinions that are negative about small business relative to large business on the jobs issue (see Table 3.2).

16. For a textbook discussion of the role of profit and the entrepreneur in a market economy, see McConnell and Brue (1999, pp. 612-614).

17. See U.S. Department of Commerce (1997). For a discussion of rates of return on equity for small businesses, see Brock and Evans (1986, pp. 32-34).

18. Elementary teachers gave significantly fewer correct estimates than did secondary teachers (28% versus 51%). In fact, more than half (53%) of elementary teachers overstated the rate of profit, and about a tenth (13%) did not know. Among middle school/junior high teachers, business-education teachers tended to give significantly more correct estimates than social studies teachers (59% versus 46%).

19. In a longitudinal study of new businesses in America, Cooper, et al. (1990) found that "most new business owners rely heavily on their own resources to finance their ventures" (p. 6). For further discussion of this issue, see *Entrepreneur* Magazine (1995, pp. 264-266).

20. This low percentage is not just due to elementary teachers. Although significantly fewer elementary teachers (13%) were aware of this typical financial source than were secondary teachers (22%), the percent correct is still low for secondary teachers. These results are also of concern because secondary teachers are the ones most likely to discuss business financing if the topic is discussed at all in the schools.

21. There were no significant differences in the ratings of females and males. A significantly greater percentage of blacks than whites (16% versus 4%) rated their knowledge and understanding as excellent, and a significantly smaller percentage of blacks than whites (12% versus 31%) rated their knowledge and understanding as poor. Hispanics were significantly more likely to

give themselves a good rating (24%) and were significantly less likely to give themselves a fair rating (29%). These results suggest that blacks and Hispanics tend to overestimate their level of knowledge and understanding of starting a business.

PLAYING BY THE RULES:
Competitive Markets and Government

Although government has an important and legitimate role to play in our market economy, many of its actions can either encourage or discourage entrepreneurship. For example, government may be impeding entrepreneurship when it intervenes in markets to establish prices, imposes onerous regulations on business or increases business taxes. Although such actions can always be debated on their *overall* merits, they are definitely not conducive to entrepreneurship. Consequently, we asked youth a set of questions designed to gauge the extent of support or non-support for an entrepreneurial environment in terms of prices, regulation and taxation.

Knowing When the Price Is Right

The results from one of the knowledge questions we asked showed that only half of youth knew the prices of most products in a competitive market were determined by supply and demand (see Table 4.3).

Of course, knowing what determines prices in a market economy and liking the outcomes that result are two different things. If demand or supply conditions change, market prices rise and fall; knowing this does not mean people will accept or like the outcome. Consequently, we decided to probe further to find out to what degree youth might be predisposed to government intervention with respect to the pricing functions of our market economy. To sample opinion, we constructed two hypothetical questions.

Putting a Ceiling on Housing Prices. The first question was: *If the supply of new houses was reduced by a shortage of lumber, do you think that the government should prohibit construction companies from raising prices on new houses?*

This topic has direct relevance to entrepreneurship because many construction companies are small businesses started by entrepreneurs. The question also was designed to provide a plausible scenario for a price increase that youth would be less likely to attribute to corporate price manipulation.

From an economics perspective, there are several reasons that might be advanced by market-oriented individuals for not interfering with the housing market's natural tendency to experience an increase in price when lumber prices rise. For example, lumber is a major cost of production for new houses. If lumber prices increase, then many home builders who operate in a competitive market would want to raise the prices of new houses in order to pay for their higher costs of production and still earn a level of profit sufficient to stay in business.

If the government were to intervene in this market and prohibit housing prices from rising, then many of these same home builders would no longer be able to cover their higher production costs without damaging their businesses' solvency or their ability to meet market demand. Again, putting aside the other issues which are often on the table when discussing price controls, such government intervention in the market's resolution of pricing would certainly be a hindrance to the pursuit of entrepreneurship.

What we found was stronger support for government action and weaker support for allowing markets to work. More than half of youth wanted the government to prohibit construction companies from raising prices on the new houses if lumber prices rose. Only about four in 10 would let the market establish housing prices.

TABLE 5.1: Government Should Prohibit Price Increases

Response	Youth	General Public	Teachers	Business Owners
	(n=1,008)	(600)	(1,609)	(204)
	%	%	%	%
Yes, prohibit	55	49	20	23
No, do not prohibit	43	4	79	77
Don't know	2	4	2	0

It is possible that youth respondents were not thinking about this market situation from an entrepreneurship or economic perspective. What they may have been thinking about was how the issue affected them as consumers (*i.e.*, having to pay a higher price for something they wanted).

Because consumers generally do not like to pay higher prices, the respondents may have thought the easiest way to solve the problem was to turn to government: "Just pass a law prohibiting companies from raising prices and the problem of rising costs is solved." Most youth appeared to be unaware of the potential negative ramifications for entrepreneurship of such interventions. History contains many examples of the unintended consequences of price controls, although most youth are probably not familiar with this history.[1]

Learning From Teachers. As we expected, the opinion of the general public was fairly similar to that of youth. About five in 10 wanted government intervention, while the rest were opposed to it. As with youth, many in the general public do not understand how prices are determined in a market economy. A large proportion of the general public may look at the economic world strictly from a consumer perspective, in which case rising prices would be perceived to have a negative effect on their welfare. In addition, government is often viewed as the primary institution for solving economic problems, so it would be natural that many would want government to intervene in the market to stop a price increase without recognizing the economic and entrepreneurship consequences.

Teachers held a different prevailing opinion: only two in 10 supported government intervention, while almost eight in 10 were opposed to it.[2] It was not surprising to find such a sharp difference between teachers and youth or the general public. Most teachers had taken one or more economics courses, so they were somewhat familiar with how the economy works. Nearly nine in 10 knew supply and demand determines the prices of most products in a market economy; most also recognized this factor and accepted it in the housing question.

The response of small-business owners was essentially the same as teachers. Two in 10 supported government intervention, while the remainder were opposed to it. Age, business experience and economic knowledge probably explain why small-business owners held this market-oriented view. The few among the owners who wanted government to set prices were probably also looking at the issue from their perspective as consumers.

Peddling Bikes for More Money

We decided to probe further to see how strong the support for competitive markets was among all groups by asking a more challenging question: *A bicycle manufacturer raises the price of bikes because the demand increased even though the cost of producing bikes has not increased. Do you think the manufacturer should be allowed to raise prices?*

What is intriguing about this question is that it shifts the factor that is driving up prices from supply to demand. The price increase comes from increased demand by consumers for the product, not from an increase in the cost of production that decreased supply.

In a market economy, there are many real-world examples of businesses raising prices based on increased demand. Hotels increase room rates, and airlines raise ticket prices during peak tourist seasons. Car manufacturers raise prices (or offer fewer discounts) for popular models. The prices of stocks and bonds increase with demand. Allowing prices to change provides incentives for the efficient use and allocation of products and resources in a market economy.

We expected responses to this question to follow the pattern established on the first question. On one hand, we expected most of youth and the general public would be opposed to allowing the bike manufacturer to raise prices, and by implication would be supporting government price intervention in this market. On the other hand, we predicted most teachers and small business owners would be opposed to placing this restriction on the entrepreneurial freedom of the manufacturer.[3] That pattern held up, as is shown in the following table.

TABLE 5.2: Manufacturer Should Be Allowed to Raise Prices

Response	Youth (n=1,008)	General Public (600)	Teachers (1,609)	Business Owners (204)
	%	%	%	%
Yes, allowed to	33	36	58	66
No, not allowed to	67	62	41	33
Don't know	1	2	1	0

One of the more interesting aspects of these results is how opposition to the market outcome increased from the first to the second question. A likely reason for this change may have been one of justification. In the first case, the price increase may have seemed more justified because it arose from a more acceptable reason for raising prices: the higher cost of doing business. In the second case, the price rose because the manufacturer experienced increased demand for a product. In this situation, it may have appeared the bike manufacturer was somehow "taking advantage" of the increased consumer interest in the product. Although both situations have the same market outcomes (higher prices) and are typical developments in a market economy, we expected more opposition to the price increase in the second situation across all groups.

The results turned out as anticipated. Among youth, just more than half were opposed to letting the market establish price in the housing case, but more than two-thirds were opposed in the bike case. The contrast in responses suggests that there was relatively weak understanding or support among some youth for how competitive markets work. It is difficult to see how youth with such attitudes will reconcile their interest in successful entrepreneurship with the preconceptions many have about the way consumer prices should be set.

The general public gave about the same response as that of

youth, most likely because, as with youth, they have limited education about business and economics and look at the world as consumers. Fewer than five in 10 expressed opposition to the price increase in the housing case, but more than six in 10 were opposed to the price increase in the bike case.

The greatest change in opinion came from teachers. Only two in 10 were opposed to the price increase in the housing case, but more than four in 10 were opposed to it in the bike case. This approximate doubling of the percentage from one case to the next was found across all teacher groups, regardless of the grade level or subject matter taught.

Small-business owners were also more opposed to allowing the price increase in the bike case than the housing case, but their opposition grew by just one in 10. This opposition remained the lowest of all groups surveyed.

Gender and Race. These two questions produced differences among subgroups of youth. For the housing case, a significantly greater percentage of females than males (58% versus 50%) thought government should prohibit the price rise. Similarly, in the bike case, a significantly greater percentage of females than males (74% versus 59%) would not allow a bike manufacturer to raise prices.

We also found a significant difference in thinking between black and white youth. On the housing question, more than six in 10 (63%) black youth wanted the government to prohibit construction companies from raising prices on the new houses, compared with only about four in 10 (45%) white youth. On the bike question, more than three-quarters (76%) of black youth would not allow the bike manufacturer to raise prices, while nearly two-thirds (65%) of white youth would not allow it.[4]

These differences show there were substantially more females than males, and blacks than whites, who disapproved of market outcomes. We don't know the reasons for these differences, but they do indicate there may be greater misunderstanding, or even mistrust, about how markets work among these groups. It may also be the case that more females and blacks were looking at the questions as consumers rather than as entrepreneurs. The challenge for the advancement of entrepreneurship among all youth will be to build greater understanding and appreciation of how markets work.[5]

The Imposing Rise of Regulation

Government imposes regulations on businesses for several reasons, including ensuring safe products for consumers, promoting worker health and safety, and protecting the environment. As with any economic decision, however, there is a trade-off: government regulations may have worthy purposes for society, but they also impose costs on businesses. In deciding whether to establish a new regulation, policy-makers must make a decision as to whether the benefits to society outweigh the regulatory costs.

The costs of new government regulations generally fall on businesses to pay—and have several effects on entrepreneurship. First, the costs can reduce the number of people willing to start a business because costs rise with the necessity of addressing government rules and regulations before producing or selling a product. Second, government regulations affect the profitability of existing businesses and can drive some into bankruptcy if they do not have the funding to comply with the regulations.

In addition, if the fixed costs of the regulation are high, then small businesses may be at a distinct disadvantage relative to larger businesses, who can spread out costs over a large scale of production.[6] It is for these reasons that businesses, especially small businesses, often complain about and oppose the imposition of burdensome new government regulations.

Time limitations prevented asking as many questions about government regulations as we would have liked. We did, however, want to get a general indication of youth's thinking about this type of government intervention in the economy. In asking the question, we are not suggesting there is a correct answer on this issue. Rather, we wanted to find out if youth held views about regulation that were similar to, or different from, those held by most entrepreneurs. The responses also serve as valuable comparisons to the positions held by youth on the topic of government price intervention.

We discovered that youth were split on the question of whether there was *too much, too little* or *about the right amount* of government regulation. More than three in 10 thought there was too much government regulation, while fewer than two in 10 thought there was too little. Thus, when youth did express an opinion in one direction or the other, they leaned toward an anti-regulatory stance. More than four in 10, however, believed there was about the right amount of government regulation, which indicates that the predominant position of youth on this issue, unlike the price-intervention issue, was basically neutral.[7]

TABLE 5.3: Government Regulation of Business

Response	Youth	General Public	Teachers	Business Owners
	(n=1,008)	(600)	(1,609)	(204)
	%	%	%	%
Too much government regulation	35	60	44	75
Too little government regulation	18	10	9	2
About the right amount of government regulation	45	25	43	21
Don't know	2	3	4	1

The Public Enemy. The general public also took an anti-regulatory position. Six in 10 felt there was too much government regulation of business, and only one in 10 thought there was too little. Only about a quarter of the general public thought there was about the right amount of government regulation.

These results differ markedly from the desire for government intervention in setting market prices in the housing and bike questions. One explanation for these seemingly contradictory responses is that the public was probably opposed to government regulation because it was not clearly apparent how the regulations would directly benefit them. They also may not have felt the need for them. In the two price questions, however, business actions taken to raise prices would adversely affect the public in their roles as consumers. In these cases, then, we would expect them to show more of a desire for government intervention to set prices.

As with youth, teachers held generally mixed views on the issue of whether there was too much, too little or about the right amount of government regulation of business. About equal percentages thought there was too much as thought there was about the right amount. Few teachers thought there was too little government regulation. Elementary teachers expressed more opposition to government regulation than other teachers. More than five in 10 elementary teachers thought there was too much government regulation, whereas only about four in 10 secondary teachers held such an opinion.

Three-fourths of small-business owners felt that there was too much government regulation of business. This response was expected, given that government regulations generally impose a cost on businesses, and business owners would be more likely to think about the cost side of the regulations than the benefit side.[8] These results stand in sharp contrast with the more neutral position of many youth, who were less certain about what side to take on the issue.

How Taxes Tax Business

Government intervenes in the economy in ways other than setting prices or regulating businesses. One of the primary forms of intervention is through taxation, which reallocates resources from the private to the public sector. From a business perspective, taxes constitute a cost of doing business and directly affect business decisions regarding employment, investment, innovation or other activities.

We wanted to get a sense of whether youth thought businesses were *overtaxed, undertaxed* or *taxed about the right amount*. Again, our intent was not to advocate one position or the other, but rather to discover the degree of opposition to this type of government intervention in the market, and to find out whether the thinking of youth was similar to or different from other groups.

The verdict was a split opinion. More than five in 10 youth believed most businesses were overtaxed, about four in 10 thought they were taxed about the right amount, and only about one in 10 felt businesses were undertaxed. The response indicates that the opinion of youth leaned toward overtaxation.[9] This opinion may just be a reflection of the negative perceptions people generally have when taxes are discussed because somebody has to pay those taxes. The responses also indicate there was greater sympathy for this business problem than might be expected among youth, given their views on government intervention in business affairs through pricing or regulation.

TABLE 5.4: Business Taxes

Response	Youth	General Public	Teachers	Business Owners
	(n=1,008)	(600)	(1,609)	(204)
	%	%	%	%
Overtaxed	51	48	29	69
Undertaxed	9	19	29	4
Taxed about the right amount	37	26	35	25
Don't know	2	7	8	1

The Rest of the Story. The general public had a reaction that was fairly similar to that of youth. About five in 10 thought businesses were overtaxed, about two in 10 thought they were undertaxed, and about a quarter thought they were taxed about the right amount. Overall, the general public appeared to manifest an anti-government stance on the taxation issue.

Teachers were almost evenly divided on the issue. About three in 10 thought they were either overtaxed, undertaxed or taxed about the right amount. This response stands in sharp contrast to that of youth and the general public. It suggests that teachers were the least concerned of any group about the impact of taxes on entrepreneurship. The response may be understandable if teachers were thinking of business taxes as a source of revenue for schools. In that case, teachers may have believed that businesses were undertaxed if they also thought that schools were underfunded.

There were several interesting differences among teachers on the degree of support for business taxation. Secondary teachers were significantly more likely than elementary teachers to think businesses were undertaxed (37% versus 25%). Among these secondary teachers, social studies teachers were significantly more likely than business educators to think businesses were undertaxed (35% versus 25%).

85

We end this chapter with a look at our fourth group: small-business owners. One would expect them to be opposed to this degree of government intervention in the economy, and they were. Almost seven in 10 thought businesses were overtaxed.

1. For a further explanation of some of the problems associated with government price controls and examples, see McConnell and Brue (1999, pp. 417-420) or most principles of economics textbooks.

2. Elementary teachers were significantly more likely than teachers at other levels to favor government price intervention (26% versus 15%).

3. There were differences in responses by teacher type in the bike case. Elementary teachers were significantly more likely (53%) to oppose the price increase than were secondary teachers (34%). At the senior high school level, business educators (34%) and other teachers (38%) were more opposed to allowing the bike manufacturer to raise prices than were social studies teachers (23%). This difference among these senior high groups had not been found in the housing case.

4. Black youth showed less knowledge about markets on one of the knowledge questions (see Table 4.3). Almost seven in 10 (69%) black youth did not recognize that most prices were determined by supply and demand compared with almost six in 10 (58%) white youth who gave incorrect answers.

5. There was no significant difference between Hispanics and other youth on the housing and bike questions.

6. For further discussion, see Brock and Evans (1986, pp. 179-180).

7. Females were significantly less likely than males (31% versus 39%) to think that there was too much government regulation, and significantly more likely to think that there was too little (21% versus 14%). About the same percentage of each group (45%-46%) thought there was the right amount of regulation. There were no significant differences in the response patterns of blacks and whites, or Hispanics and other youth on the issue of government regulation.

8. They view government regulation as a burden because it makes it more difficult to start a business (see Table 3.5).

9. The perceptions of females and males, blacks and whites, and Hispanics and other youth were about the same on the issue of business taxation.

SPREADING THE WEALTH:
Philanthropy and Entrepreneurship

Beyond the Bottom Line

Successful business owners or entrepreneurs make both economic and philanthropic contributions to the communities in which they live. The former includes increasing jobs, expanding business activity and paying taxes to support government. Philanthropic contributions are made in many other ways,

including giving to non-profit organizations, establishing charitable foundations, doing public service work and serving as
advisers or role models.

Yet, because entrepreneurs may be thought of as people who
simply start businesses and create wealth, the contributions they
make to the community are often overlooked. Much of the focus
in the news media and in books is on how entrepreneurs become
successful, the companies they create or the lifestyles they lead.
Less attention is given to what entrepreneurs do for the economy
and their communities when businesses become successful—
and still less is written about what entrepreneurs do with their
wealth and their time after they have "made it."[1]

How do America's youth view this situation? Do they think
people start businesses to become rich, and then just hold onto
their money? Are they aware of a connection between doing
well for oneself as an entrepreneur and doing "good" for the
community? Do they realize a successful business creates many
jobs, invests in a community and also pays taxes that support
government at all levels (local, state and federal)? Do they recognize how often a large proportion of wealth generated from
entrepreneurship is put back into a community through charitable activities?

To further explore youth's understanding of philanthropy,
another survey was given to a national sample of youth and
younger adults, ages 14 to 39. To maintain consistency with previous analyses, responses are reported from the target audience,
youth from ages 14 to 19. To offer a contrast, responses are also
reported from a sample of adults ages 29 to 39. In many respects,
this adult sample could be considered a slice of the general public,
a group which was used in earlier comparisons.[2]

Noticing Community Contributions

First, an open-ended question was asked to find out if youth could even identify the contributions that business owners or entrepreneurs made to the community where they were located. About a quarter cited economic factors, such as providing jobs, adding to the economy (money, goods or services) or paying taxes. Just more than one in 10 recognized the philanthropic activities of business owners or entrepreneurs, such as contributing to or establishing charities and foundations, doing public service work, giving advice or serving as role models.

TABLE 6.1: Contribute to Community

Response	Youth (n=359)	Adults (450)
	%	%
Economic factors	25	49
Provide jobs	14	34
Contribute to economy	9	9
Pay taxes	2	6
Philanthropic factors	13	17
Give to/Establish charities	4	7
Do public service work	7	8
Be role model/Give advice	2	2
Other	6	6
Nothing	9	9
Don't know	47	19

Our initial suspicion that most youth would not recognize the contribution made to the community by entrepreneurs was confirmed by the size of the "don't know" response. Almost half of the sample could not think of a single contribution business owners or entrepreneurs made to their local community! Another one in 10 said entrepreneurs contributed "nothing." These results indicate that youth fail to make the connection between entrepreneurship and philanthropy.

How did adults respond relative to youth? They were clearly more aware of what entrepreneurs contribute to a community. Almost five in 10 identified an economic contribution, and nearly two in 10 noted a philanthropic contribution made by successful business owners and entrepreneurs. Far fewer adults (fewer than two in 10) than youth (five in 10) gave a "don't know" response.

How Much Is Enough?

Next, we noted for each respondent the two major economic contributions successful entrepreneurs provide to the community: providing jobs and paying taxes. We then asked whether that contribution was enough, or whether they should give more. The intent in asking this question was to find out if youth thought most successful entrepreneurs were meeting their obligations (as perceived by youth) to help the community.

Youth had a split opinion on the question of community responsibility of successful entrepreneurs. Half thought they should give more, but almost half also thought they gave enough.

By contrast, adults saw less of a need for a philanthropic contribution. Many adults held the position that successful business owners and entrepreneurs gave enough to the community by providing jobs and paying taxes and should not be obligated to give more. Six in 10 adults held this view, whereas fewer than three in 10 thought successful business owners and entrepreneurs should give more to the community.

TABLE 6.2: Contribute Enough to Community

Response	Youth (n=359)	Adults (450)
	%	%
Contribute enough	45	61
Should give more	51	29
Should give less	0	2
Depends	2	5
Don't know/Refused	2	3

The question was also asked in a slightly different way to explore for correspondence in the responses. The second question was: *How important do you think it is for successful business owners or entrepreneurs to contribute something to the community beyond providing jobs or paying taxes?*

When the responsibility issue was phrased in this way, about half of youth thought it was very important. The other half thought it was only somewhat important. About the same percentage of adults as youth thought it was very important. A slightly smaller percentage of adults than youth thought it was somewhat important, but that's because one in 10 adults also thought it was not important at all.

TABLE 6.3:   Importance of Giving Something Back to the Community

Response	Youth (n=359)	Adults (450)
	%	%
Very important	46	48
Somewhat important	50	39
Not at all important	4	11
Don't know	—	2

The way we interpret the responses to the two similar questions is that youth hold ambivalent attitudes toward the philanthropic responsibilities of successful business owners or entrepreneurs. Many would like business owners or entrepreneurs to give more to the community and think such actions are important. Others, however, think entrepreneurs give enough and consider civic responsibility to be of somewhat lesser importance. Adults are less split in their opinions than youth. They appear to be less demanding of successful business owners and entrepreneurs, and attach less importance to their civic responsibility.

Give Us One Good Reason . . .

A list of possible reasons also was developed dealing with why a business owner or entrepreneur might contribute to a community. We then asked youth to state whether each was a major reason, a minor reason or not a reason to contribute. Reporting focused on the major reasons because they best tell the story.

Youth thought that the major reasons for contributions to the community from business owners or entrepreneurs arose from both altruistic and selfish motives. The altruistic reason drawing the most support—from more than three-fourths of youth—was that business owners or entrepreneurs made contributions because they wanted to help the community. Another altruistic reason cited by half of youth was a personal belief in voluntary giving.

94

TABLE 6.4: Reasons to Contribute to Community

Response	Youth (n=359)	Adults (450)
	%	%
Want to help community	77	72
Want to promote their business	61	73
Personal belief in voluntary giving	51	56
Want name remembered	42	64
It is tax deductible	42	51
The government requires it	37	26

There was also support for several selfish motives, but it was not as strong as those indicating altruistic reasons. About six in 10 youth thought that successful business owners and entrepreneurs gave to the community in order to promote a business. About four in 10 believed that wanting your name remembered was a major reason for giving.

According to most youth, government policies were not a major motivating factor for why business owners or entrepreneurs gave to the community. Just more than four in 10 cited the tax deductibility of contributions as a major reason for giving, while just fewer than four in 10 were of the belief that the major reason for contributions was that the government required it. Because there is no government requirement for such giving, the latter response shows that more than a third of youth had no idea why business owners or entrepreneurs really contribute to a community.

Adults were more cynical in their views of the motives for giving. Significantly higher percentages of adults than youth thought the major reasons were to promote their business, to want their name remembered or to lower taxes. Not all adults, however, thought the reasons were selfish ones. About the same percentage of adults as youth cited "wanting to help the community" or a "personal belief in voluntary giving" as major reasons why business owners or entrepreneurs contributed to the community.

Ways and Means

Successful business owners or entrepreneurs can give to communities in many ways. They can make charitable contributions or establish a charitable foundation. They can serve as volunteers for a local charity or do public service work. They can also provide greater economic benefits to their employees. To find out which of these options were considered more important by youth, we gave them a list of four ways contributions can be made and asked them to evaluate each one on a five-point scale that ranged from "very important" to "not at all important."

TABLE 6.5: Importance of Ways to Contribute to Community

Response	Youth (n=359)	Adults (450)
	%	%
Contributions to local charities	82	63
Provide better benefits or services for employees	79	75
Work as volunteer for local charity or on a public service project	67	53
Start new charity or charitable foundation	64	36

The two ways that received the most support among youth—with about eight in 10 saying each was either "important" or "very important"—was "contributing to local charities" and "providing better benefits and services for employees." The other two options were less popular. The idea of having a business owner or entrepreneur work as a volunteer for a local charity or work on a public service project was appealing to two-thirds of youth. A slightly smaller percentage thought starting a new charity or charitable foundation was of importance.

Adults were significantly less supportive than youth of three of the four options. Only about a third thought starting a new charity or charitable foundation was of importance. Only about half thought it was "important" or "very important" for business owners or entrepreneurs to volunteer for a charity or work on a public service project. Just more than six in 10 thought it was worthwhile for successful business owners or entrepreneurs to make contributions to local charities. The only way in which youth and adults showed strong agreement was providing better benefits or services for employees.

Building the Foundation

For the final survey question on philanthropy, we decided to probe for knowledge about charitable foundations. This seemed a natural progression, as the history of philanthropy in the United States shows most large charitable foundations were started with significant endowments by successful entrepreneurs. Andrew Carnegie, Henry Ford, John D. Rockefeller, W. W. Kellogg, J. Howard Pew, Alfred P. Sloan, Charles Stewart Mott and Ewing Marion Kauffman are but a few who have earned this distinction.[3]

As we expected, few youth understood the important relationship between entrepreneurship and philanthropy. Just more than a third correctly knew that most large charitable foundations were started by large contributions from successful entrepreneurs. Almost half thought they were started by small contributions from many individuals. About one in 10 even believed that large charitable foundations were started by the legislative actions of federal, state or local government.

TABLE 6.6: Who Starts Charitable Foundations?

Response	Youth (n=359)	Adults (450)
	%	%
*Large contributions from successful business owners or entrepreneurs	35	39
Legislative action of federal government or state and local government	18	12
Small contributions from many individuals	45	45
Don't know/Other	3	3

*Correct Response

These surveys show there is clearly a great deal of confusion and misinformation in the minds of youth about philanthropy in the United States. Further, we believe the connection between what entrepreneurs have to do to *become* successful and what they often do *after* they become successful is an important part of entrepreneurship education. That's why the focus of the following chapter is on education, a means of offering another career option for those who want to help their communities: becoming a successful entrepreneur.

1. Few books on entrepreneurship discuss philanthropy. See Drucker (1985), Maddox (1995) or Ericksen (1997) for examples.

2. We were not able to survey teachers, small-business owners or the general public on these philanthropy questions because of limited resources. The size of this youth sample was 359. The maximum margin of sampling error was +/- 5.2% at the 95 percent level of confidence. The size of the adult sample was 450. The maximum margin of sampling error was +/- 4.6%.

3. For a history of philanthropy in the United States, see Bremner (1988).

TAKING A LESSON:
Entrepreneurship Education

In Chapter 4, we reported the results from our testing of youth's basic knowledge with respect to small business, entrepreneurship and economics—results which revealed substantial gaps in knowledge, as the typical youth could answer fewer than half the test questions on our survey. In addition, most youth were well aware of their knowledge deficiencies. Almost five in 10 gave themselves a "poor" or "very poor" rating on their knowledge and understanding of starting and managing a business. Another three in 10 gave themselves only a "fair" rating.

Looking for the Silver Lining

The silver lining in these results is that at least there is a strong correspondence between what youth appear to know and what they *think* they know on these topics.

The youth we interviewed did not have an inflated opinion of their knowledge and did not deny that they had a knowledge problem. Instead, their self-assessment openly (and correctly) revealed weaknesses in their understanding of how business works.

Why were youth knowledge scores and self-assessments so low? What factors contributed to these conditions among youth? To probe these intriguing questions and examine a potential source of the problem, we turn now to the results for the survey questions on entrepreneurship and economic education of youth.[1]

Coursework, of Course

We began our series of education questions with a focus on the most obvious factor—courses taken. We wanted to know to what extent youth took courses in business or entrepreneurship, and how many took courses in economics. Such courses help provide the foundation for understanding how entrepreneurship and the economy work.

We would not expect most students to know much about these

topics if they had not received some formal education on the topics in school. A few may learn about how entrepreneurship or the economy works from their parents, family, friends, role models and work experiences. However, they are the exception and not the norm. Most youth do not have access to entrepreneurship and economic education from informal sources, so formal education is critical for the development of their basic knowledge and understanding.

What we found was that just more than a quarter of youth said they had taken a course in business or entrepreneurship in high school.[2] This result represents a lost opportunity with respect to the education of high school students. We know from the earlier survey questions that the great majority of high school students expressed interest in starting a business or showed entrepreneurial inclinations, yet their formal education failed to provide the understanding or knowledge that would help develop or encourage those interests. One can only wonder what additional opportunities the future might have held for these youth and the nation had their education been more complete.

TABLE 7.1: Courses Taken in High School

Courses	Youth (n=1,008)	General Public (600)	Owners (204)
	%	%	%
Business or Entrepreneurship	27	25	26
Economics	35	39	38

We discovered the same problem with course-taking in economics. Only about a third of youth reported they had taken an economics course in high school.[3] An economics course can be extraordinarily helpful for understanding how prices and wages are determined in a market economy, how resources and products get allocated among producers and consumers, and how the macroeconomy affects consumption, investment and production decisions. Despite its importance, about two-thirds of youth failed to receive any formal education in economics.[4] The result of this situation is that youth learn little about economics in school and must learn about the economy on their own. This problem can lead to miseducation about numerous topics, as suggested by the many incorrect responses by youth to our knowledge questions on economics.

Mirror Images Among Adults. The high school education of the general public and small-business owners in business and economics was not much different from that of youth. Only about a quarter of both groups had taken a course in business or entrepreneurship. Fewer than four in 10 had taken a high school course in economics.

These percentages also indicate that most of the general public and most small-business owners had little or no education in entrepreneurship or economics when they graduated from high school and were probably ill-prepared to start a business at that time. We can only speculate about what would have happened to these groups if more formal education had been provided, but we suspect that many more businesses may have been started by younger entrepreneurs.

In the knowledge test given to all groups, the general public scored slightly higher than youth, and small-business owners scored significantly higher (see Table 4.1). We were curious about how both small-business owners and the general public could score higher, given their similar type of high school education in business and economics. One probable explanation for the differences may be the impact of courses taken in college.

Eight in 10 small-business owners we surveyed reported that they attended college. Among this group, almost seven in 10 took courses in general business management or economics. Also, more than a third of this group had taken a course in small business or entrepreneurship. Among the general public, more than four in 10 stated they had attended college. Among this group, about half took courses in general business or economics, and a quarter took a course in small business or entrepreneurship. This additional education, plus their business or work experience, are the more likely reasons why the general public—and especially small-business owners—showed significantly more knowledge about entrepreneurship and the economy than did youth.

Teachers' Education. We were also interested in the entrepreneurship and economic education of teachers, in part because this information might give us insights as to how prepared educators were to teach topics in entrepreneurship and economics. The teachers we surveyed had all attended college, such attendance being a requirement for obtaining certification to teach in the schools.

We first asked about courses on small business and entrepreneurship, because this factor may affect preparation for teaching about entrepreneurship in the school curriculum. Fewer than two in 10 (18%) teachers reported taking an undergraduate or a graduate course in small-business or entrepreneurship. This course taking varied by grade level and subject taught. Fewer than one in 10 (9%) elementary teachers took such a course, but more than two in 10 (24%) secondary teachers had taken such a course. As might be expected, significantly more business education teachers had completed a small business or entrepreneurship course compared to social studies teachers (41% versus 14%).

A course in economics helps provide background for understanding competitive markets and how the economy works. Most teachers reported that they had taken a course in economics, but again, course taking varied by grade level and subject taught. Almost eight in 10 secondary teachers had taken an economics course, compared with only about six in 10 elementary teachers. At the secondary level, business education teachers were significantly more likely than social studies teachers to have taken an economics course (94% versus 80%).

What the course-taking percentages for teachers suggest is that those teachers most likely to teach about entrepreneurship or the economy—secondary teachers in business education or social studies—have some degree of preparation for teaching these topics. What we don't know is the complete extent of their preparation or how well they teach about these topics.

Based on teacher test scores and teacher self-ratings (see Tables 4.1 and 4.3), we suspect it could be better. Thus, lack of teacher knowledge and poor access to education in entrepreneurship and economics are both probable contributing factors to the low knowledge scores and self-assessments of youth in these areas.

Well, What Do You Know?

Although we discovered most youth had not taken a course in entrepreneurship or economics, we also wanted to check if our results were consistent with youth's assessment of their education in those subjects. We expected those youth without course work would give us a negative assessment of their education, and thought many of those who had taken entrepreneurship or economics courses might offer a similar assessment because the quality and content of such courses can vary.

We asked a question that gave youth a list of subjects or topics to consider so we could make comparisons among different subjects: mathematics, science, literature, U.S. history, government, economics and business. We also gave them three options to describe their education in those subjects or topics—*a lot, a little,* or *nothing at all.* The responses of youth provide some interesting contrasts.

What was especially striking were the very low ratings given to both economics and business. Almost nine in 10 said they were taught little or nothing about how business works. Similarly, almost eight in 10 reported being taught little or nothing at all about how the economy works.[5] Both percentages are consistent with the fact that only a minority take a high school course in entrepreneurship or economics and with the assumption that students do not think they learn much from such courses when they do take them. These high percentages contrast sharply with the low percentages for "little or nothing" given for other subjects.

TABLE 7.2: Amount of Education on Subjects (n=1,008 youth)

Response	A Lot	A Little	Nothing
	%	%	%
Mathematics	94	6	1
English or American literature	84	15	1
Science	84	14	2
United States history	76	21	3
How the federal government works	33	56	11
How the economy works	23	63	13
How business works	15	66	19

Strong Opinions on Strengthening Education

We have reported that most youth do not take courses in entrepreneurship and economics, and that they perceive they are taught little or nothing in school about how business or the economy works. In another question, we sought to discover what youth thought of the importance of their schools' teaching students about entrepreneurship and starting a business. Given the strong interest in entrepreneurship expressed by youth in a previous question (see Table 2.1),  we were not surprised by their positive response— only by the strength of the sentiment.

Youth overwhelmingly thought the nation's schools should do more to teach about entrepreneurship and starting a business. Almost eight in 10 considered entrepreneurship and starting a business to be *important* or *very important* for the schools to teach.[6] Youth appeared to recognize a connection between their knowledge problems and low self-ratings and the need for more entrepreneurship education in the schools.

TABLE 7.3:   Nation's Schools Should Teach about Entrepreneurship and Starting a Business

Item and Response	Youth	General Public	Teachers	Business Owners
	(n=1,008)	(600)	(1,609)	(204)
	%	%	%	%
5 (Very important)	44	60	46	61
4	33	22	35	20
3	18	13	16	16
2	3	2	3	3
1 (Not at all important)	2	3	0	0
Don't know	0	1	0	0

The general public and small-business owners expressed views similar to youth. More than eight in 10 of these groups considered entrepreneurship and starting a business to be *important* or *very important* for schools to teach. In fact, these groups expressed this opinion even more strongly than youth. Six in 10 of the general public and small business owners thought these topics were *very important*.

The great majority of teachers also thought entrepreneurship and starting a business were *important* or *very important* for schools to teach. More than eight in 10 shared the sentiment. Teachers, however, did not hold quite as strong an opinion on this issue as the general public or small-business owners. A significantly smaller percentage thought the subject was *very important*, and more teachers were likely to rate it as *important*. Nevertheless, the overall opinion of teachers was still very positive and almost identical to that held by youth.[7]

Why Subject Matter Matters

We thought it would be of value to find out what small-business owners and teachers thought about topics in entrepreneurship that need to be taught to high school students. Our reason for making this comparison was to see if the views of teachers were similar to those of small-business owners. We asked both groups about the knowledge, skills and attitudes or values related to entrepreneurship that should be taught to youth.

Important Knowledge. In the knowledge domain, financial management was thought to be *important* or *very important* for a high school senior's knowledge of entrepreneurship by more than nine in 10 small-business owners. More than eight in 10 felt the same about instruction on the topics of marketing, sales and advertising. About three-fourths thought that product costing and pricing were *important* or *very important* to teach. Fewer than six in 10, however, thought instruction in basic business law was *important* or *very important* for knowledge of entrepreneurship.

The overall perspective of teachers was strikingly similar to the opinions of small-business owners. In fact, they had the same rank order for the topics in terms of their importance: financial management, marketing, sales and advertising, product costing and pricing, and basic business law. The major difference between the views of teachers and small-business owners was on the topic of business law, which both groups considered less essential, but small-business owners more so than teachers.

TABLE 7.4:   Importance of Entrepreneurship Topics to a High School Senior's Education*

Response	Teachers (n=1,609)	Business Owners (204)
	%	%
A. Knowledge		
Product costing and pricing	82	77
Marketing, sales and advertising	84	84
Financial management	95	92
Basic business law	76	59

Continued on next page

Response	Teachers	Business Owners
B. Skills		
Assessing market opportunities	87	84
Developing a business plan	87	91
Analyzing a financial statement	88	76
Accounting and record keeping	91	79
Motivating and managing people	93	91
C. Attitudes and Values		
Business ethics	97	88
Leadership	97	95
Team work	96	92
Risk-taking	84	76
Persistence	94	89

*Percent saying important or very important.

Developing Skills. The development of skills is necessary for preparing high school students to become successful entrepreneurs. More than nine in 10 small-business owners believed it was either *important* or *very important* to teach high school students how to motivate and manage people. The same high percentage also thought it was *important* or *very important* to provide instruction in developing a business plan. Eight in 10 believed assessing market opportunities was *important* or *very important* to teach, while fewer than eight in 10 accorded the same status to accounting and record keeping or analyzing financial statements.

A comparison of the views of teachers and small-business owners on skills development showed strong similarities. Like small-business owners, nine in 10 teachers considered it *very important* or *important* for high school seniors to learn about managing and motivating people. Almost nine in 10 thought teaching skills related to developing a business plan or assessing market opportunities was *important* or *very important*. A higher percentage of teachers than small-business owners, however, attached importance to analyzing financial statements or learning about accounting and record keeping as skills for preparing high school seniors to become entrepreneurs.

Attitudes and Values. A third potential topic for an entrepreneurship curriculum in high schools is the teaching of attitudes and values. About nine in 10 small-business owners believed the following attitudes or values were *important* or *very important* to teach for preparing high school seniors for entrepreneurship: leadership, teamwork, persistence and business ethics. The lowest-rated topic was risk-taking. Even so, three-fourths of small-business owners thought this attitude was *important* or *very important* for a school curriculum in entrepreneurship.

Teachers felt more strongly than small-business owners about the importance of each of the five attitudes or values. More than 90 percent of teachers considered it either *very important* or *important* to teach about leadership, business ethics, teamwork and persistence. More than eight in 10 felt the same about risk-taking. The two topics on which teachers and small-business owners showed the most difference were business ethics and risk-taking.[8]

The conclusion that can be drawn from these curriculum-related comparisons is that there is a great deal of consistency in the views of teachers and small-business owners about what should be taught about entrepreneurship in high school. The real challenge for entrepreneurship education is to improve youth access to such education as well as the entrepreneurship focus of the topics covered—issues we discuss in our concluding chapter.

1. For other discussions of entrepreneurship education, see Kent (1990), Kourilsky (1995), and Kourilsky and Carlson (1997).

2. The differences in the responses of females and males (29% versus 26%), or blacks and whites (33% versus 28%), about taking a business or entrepreneurship course in high school were small. Hispanics, however, were significantly less likely than others (19% versus 29%) to have taken such a course.

3. A significantly greater percentage of blacks than whites (45% versus 34%) said they took an economics course. A slightly smaller percentage of Hispanics (30%) than whites or blacks reported taking an economics course, but these differences were not significant. Also, a slightly greater percentage of females than males (36% versus 32%) said they took an economics course, but the differences were not significant.

4. The most likely reason that the percentage for economics is higher than that for business courses is that economics is a mandated course for high school students to take in some states. These courses, however, vary in coverage. Some focus on basic economics, while others cover consumer economics, and still others combine economics and government topics. For a discussion of course-taking patterns in economics or business courses in American high schools over the years, see Walstad (1994b, pp. 109-136).

5. There were no significant differences between females and males in the perceptions about the amount of education on business and the economy. A substantially smaller percentage of blacks than whites (77% versus 85%) believed that they were taught little or nothing about how business works. Blacks were also significantly less likely than whites (70% versus 79%) to say they were taught a lot about how the economy works. Hispanics were significantly less likely (64%) than others to state that they were taught little or nothing about how the economy works. Despite these differences, large percentages of each group felt they were taught little or nothing about how either business or the economy works.

6. Blacks were significantly more likely than whites to consider the teaching of entrepreneurship to be very important (67% versus 38%) and significantly less likely to think it was just important (17% versus 37%). There was essentially no difference between the views of Hispanics and others. There was also no significant difference between the views of females and males.

7.   The opinion of teachers was almost the same, regardless of the grade level taught. Among secondary teachers, business educators were significantly more likely to think that teaching about entrepreneurship was important or very important (89%) than were other teachers, but you would expect this to be the case, given their special interest in entrepreneurship as a topic in business-education courses.

8.   There were only minor differences among teacher groups by grade level or subject taught on the importance of the knowledge, skills, or attitudes and values to be included in an entrepreneurship curriculum for senior high students.

REACHING CONCLUSIONS:
Youth and Entrepreneurship

Any effort at reporting an extensive amount of survey data carries with it the peril of getting lost in the numbers and missing central messages. To circumvent this potential problem, we begin this chapter with a brief summary of several key findings. It is also clear that simply reporting results offers an incomplete picture of youth and entrepreneurship; some interpretation must be attached to infuse the findings with meaning. To this end, several important implications for entrepreneurship in the United States are discussed in the second part of the chapter.

Six Major Findings

1. **Strong Interest in Starting a Business.** Entrepreneurial interest among youth in the United States is strong. About two-thirds said they wanted to start a business of their own. The primary reason given was to *be your own boss* and *control your life*. Earning lots of money was not considered to be a major motivating factor for starting a business. The primary reason for not wanting to start a business was a feeling that something was lacking—energy, ideas, education or confidence.

2. **Positive Views of Small Business.** Youth held positive opinions about small business compared to large corporations. If given a choice, a majority of youth (as well as most of the general public and most teachers) would rather be the owner of a small business than the manager of a large corporation. What youth especially liked about small business was customer service and employee relations. Despite these positive views, many do not have a personal connection with a small-business owner who might serve as a role model for entrepreneurship later in life, nor do they have a full appreciation for the challenges facing entrepreneurs.

3. **Deficiencies in Entrepreneurial Knowledge.** There were many deficiencies in the knowledge of youth about entrepreneurship, business and economics. Fewer than half could answer basic questions on these topics. Based on their self-assessments, however, youth were aware these deficiencies existed. More than four in 10 rated their business knowledge *very poor* or *poor;* another

four in 10 rated their knowledge as only *fair*. Fewer than two in 10 would give themselves a *good* or *excellent* rating. Youth may not know much about entrepreneurship, business and economics, but they do know they need more education.

4. Opinions on Markets and Government. Many youth felt there is too much regulation and taxation of business by government. This support for business, however, depended on how issues affected them as consumers. A large majority also wanted the government to intervene in particular markets to prevent consumers from having to pay higher prices for particular products. Most were resistant to normal market mechanisms for adjusting price to reflect variations in costs of material and labor.

5. Failing to Identify Philanthropy. Youth showed a lack of knowledge of the relationship between entrepreneurship and the community. Only about half could identify an economic or philanthropic contribution made by entrepreneurs to the community. Only a third were aware that most large charitable foundations in the United States were started by substantial contributions from successful business owners or entrepreneurs. However, although many youth were unaware of what entrepreneurs do for their community, they believed successful business owners and entrepreneurs had a responsibility to give back to their communities.

6. Recognizing the Importance of Education. Given the limited access of youth to entrepreneurship education and entrepreneurial role models, low knowledge scores and self-ratings were not surprising. Only about a quarter reported taking courses in entrepreneurship or business, and only about a third reported taking an economics course in high school. In addition, courses categorized as "basic business" or "economics" contained little core content of entrepreneurship. Yet, youth—as well as the other population groups surveyed—nonetheless had strong opinions about education. More than three-fourths felt it was *very important* or *important* for the nation's schools to teach more about entrepreneurship and starting a business.

Important Implications

We find the entrepreneurial mind of America's youth to be full of dreams, desires and energy, and optimistic about the prospects of starting a business and taking control of one's own destiny. At the same time, it is a mind full of misperceptions, self-doubt and frustration, lacking an understanding of how business and the economy works—yet yearning to know more.

These contrasts mean many youth who want to become entrepreneurs may never be able to realize their dreams. They do not have the necessary knowledge or skills to act on them; they are missing the role models or personal relationships to see what it means to be a successful entrepreneur; and they lack the encouragement needed to undertake a new venture. For any or all of these reasons, entrepreneurial interest among youth may never be transformed into either the creation of new businesses or the manifestation of entrepreneurial thinking within an existing venture.

Opportunity Lost. A distinct personal loss can result. Youth who want to control their destiny, or at least make the attempt, never have the opportunity to do so. Those who want to become their own boss and take charge of their lives may never have the support they need to put themselves in the position to do so. For the entrepreneurially inclined, this situation can increase personal frustration and produce lifelong regret, generating beliefs such as, "If only I'd acted on my dreams, I'd be different today."

There is also a loss for the nation. Businesses that might have been started do not get started. Ideas that would benefit consumers never get developed into goods and services and tried out in the marketplace. Economic and philanthropic contributions to communities that would have been made by successful entrepreneurs do not get made. A potential means for increasing economic growth at the local, state and national levels is never fully realized.

This is not to say that all, or even most, youth must become entrepreneurs. It is to suggest, however, that there is much greater interest in and potential for entrepreneurship in this nation, especially among youth, than has been realized to date. But, the significant demand by youth for entrepreneurship education is not being met. If significantly more youth received the education and encouragement that would enable them to become successful entrepreneurs at some point in their lives, then there would be a significant increase in the

entrepreneurial human capital of the nation. Such a contribution would improve long-term economic growth in the nation, benefit consumers, aid communities and increase the self-fulfillment of individuals.

Even those youth who do not become entrepreneurs may benefit from exposure to entrepreneurship. The knowledge, skills and attitudes that serve as its foundation are directly applicable to many situations at work and home. Thus, entrepreneurship education can be put to good use in whatever career path is chosen and better prepare youth for dealing with life's changes. It also has the potential for making the work environment more entrepreneurial in businesses and public institutions.

Finally, entrepreneurship education for youth can significantly improve diversity within the ranks of America's entrepreneurs. Six in 10 female, seven in 10 Hispanic and almost eight in 10 black youth surveyed were interested in starting businesses of their own. If more ways could be found to encourage and support this interest, both the nation and local communities would benefit from more businesses being started and owned by women and minorities.

Education Found. While there are clear benefits to encouraging greater entrepreneurship among youth, the question remains as to how it can be most effectively done.

When it comes to entrepreneurship education, what most students receive is simply inadequate. Too few are taking the course work that gives them sufficient knowledge to understand the entrepreneurial process and its underlying economic principles. This condition helps explain why many believe they learn little or nothing about these topics in school. Test scores also show that youth lack knowledge of the basic concepts related to entrepreneurship, business and the economy. It is thus not surprising they lack confidence in their knowledge and understanding of starting a business.

What needs to be done is for schools to take a closer look at curricula and respond to the overwhelming demand for entrepreneurship education by youth, teachers, the general public and the business community. The great majority of youth and the other groups surveyed characterized it as *very important* or *important* for the nation's schools to teach more about entrepreneurship and starting a business.

Ways also must be found to increase the percentage of students taking courses that include entrepreneurship content, whether they are found in business departments, social studies departments or in after-school venues. New courses are not necessarily required. In light of today's crowded curricula, an effective way for schools to provide this important education is to integrate entrepreneurship concepts into existing courses.

Part of this education means giving more emphasis to the knowledge, skills and thought processes of entrepreneurship that both small-business owners and teachers agree are important to be taught by the time a student graduates from high school. Other areas deserving of emphasis are the linkage between entrepreneurship and community philanthropy, and ethical issues which arise in the context of entrepreneurship. As already suggested, this kind of education benefits the budding entrepreneur and is also of value to those who choose other career paths. Effective education in entrepreneurship has broad application and is not simply specialized training for those who believe they want to become entrepreneurs.

There also needs to be better sequential coordination in the school curriculum for the teaching of entrepreneurship. This learning opportunity needs to be included in a systematic fashion from kindergarten through 12th grade. Why wait for senior high school to teach entrepreneurship, when interest is being manifested at much earlier ages?

Helping Hands. Many people can help in this effort to get more entrepreneurship taught in the schools. Because teachers are key to determining what actually gets taught in the classroom, they need to be better prepared (through teacher education and other means) to deal with topics related to entrepreneurship, business and economics. Armed with the increased confidence this preparation can supply, teachers will be more likely to present and convey effectively entrepreneurship concepts in the classroom.

Currently, entrepreneurship may be taught variously in social studies, business education or vocational education departments within schools. This is problematic; the topic should not be taught in piecemeal fashion. Teachers and administrators need to discuss with each other what is being taught where, so there is effective coverage and reinforcement of education on essential concepts across all units.

School counselors can be effective partners in this process, too, by recognizing that becoming an entrepreneur is a viable career path for many youth. Only then can they help those who are interested achieve their objectives. Educational strategies they can develop might include providing information about relevant high school coursework, matching students with appropriate youth organizations and entrepreneur mentors, providing support for establishing Internet communication channels with existing entrepreneurs, and sourcing internship opportunities with community entrepreneurs and support organizations.

Parents also can make contributions to the entrepreneurship education of youth. First, they may need to rethink their view of jobs and occupations, acknowledging that becoming an entrepreneur is indeed one of the possible career avenues for their children to pursue. Next, they should encourage their children who do have a dream of starting their own business by making connections with entrepreneurs in their communities who can serve as role models—or simply by discussing with their children what small businesses do in a community.

Finally, entrepreneurs and successful business owners can provide inspiration and support. They can volunteer to help the schools restructure the curriculum to give more emphasis to entrepreneurship. They can serve as role models and mentors when they discuss with teachers and students the rewards and obstacles of becoming an entrepreneur. They can share their experiences and offer entrepreneurship education internships for youth within their companies.

For the benefit of our youth, as well as our entire society, we must focus our resources on enhancing the educational conditions that nurture the entrepreneurial spark. If we can succeed in this effort, the personal and social rewards for all will be great.

REFERENCES

Bernstein, D. (1992). *Better Than a Lemonade Stand: Small Business Ideas for Kids.* Hillsboro, Oregon: Beyond Words Publishing.

Bremner, R.H. (1988). *American Philanthropy.* Chicago: University of Chicago Press.

Brock, W.A. & Evans, D.S. (1986). *The Economics of Small Businesses: Their Role and Regulation in the U.S. Economy.* New York: Holmes and Meier.

Cooper, A.C., Dunkelberg, W.C., Woo, C.Y., & Dennis, W.J. (1990). *New Business in America: The Firms and Their Owners.* Washington, D.C.: The NFIB Foundation.

Dennis, W.J. (1993). *A Small Business Primer.* Washington, D.C.: The NFIB Foundation.

Development Associates, Inc. (1993). "Awareness and Attitudes of Minority Youth and Young Adults Toward Business Ownership." Report for the Minority Business Development Agency, United States Department of Commerce.

Drucker, P.F. (1985). *Innovation and Entrepreneurship: Practice and Principles.* New York: Harper and Row.

Entrepreneur Magazine. (1995). "Small Business Advisor." New York: John Wiley.

Ericksen, G.K. (1997). *What's Luck Got to Do With It?: 12 Entrepreneurs Reveal The Secrets Behind Their Success.* New York: John Wiley.

Green, S. & Pryde, P. (1990). *Black Entrepreneurship in America.* New Brunswick: Transactions Publishers.

124

Kent, C. (ed.). (1990). *Entrepreneurship Education: Current Development, Future Directions.* New York: Quorum Books.

Kourilsky, M.L. (1990). "Entrepreneurial Thinking and Behavior: What Role the Classroom?" In C. Kent (ed.), *Entrepreneurship Education: Current Developments, Future Directions* (pp. 137-152). New York: Quorum Books.

Kourilsky, M.L. (1995). "Entrepreneurship Education: Opportunity in Search of Curriculum." *Business Education Forum,* 50(10): 11-15.

Kourilsky, M.L. (1998). "Marketable Skills for an Entrepreneurial Economy." White paper. Kansas City, MO: Kauffman Center for Entrepreneurial Leadership at the Ewing Marion Kauffman Foundation.

Kourilsky, M.L., Allen, C., Bocage, A., & Waters, G. (1995). *The New Youth Entrepreneur* (12 volumes). Camden, N. J.: Education, Training & Enterprise Center Inc.

Kourilsky, M.L. & Carlson, S. (1997). "Entrepreneurship Education for Youth: A Curricular Perspective." In D. Sexton and R. Smilor (eds.), *Entrepreneurship 2000,* (pp. 193-213). Chicago, IL: Upstart Publishing Company.

Kourilsky, M.L. & Esfandiari, M. (1997). "Entrepreneurship Education and Lower Socioeconomic Black Youth: An Empirical Investigation." *The Urban Review,* 29(3): 205-215.

Kourilsky, M.L. & Walstad, W.B. (1998). "Entrepreneurship and Female Youth: Knowledge, Attitudes, Gender Differences, and Educational Practices." *Journal of Business Venturing,* 13(1): 77-88.

Kuratko, D.F. & Hodgtetts, R.M. (1998). *Entrepreneurship: A Contemporary Approach* (4th ed.). Ft. Worth: The Dryden Press.

Lambing, P. and Kuehl, C. (1997). *Entrepreneurship.* Upper Saddle River, New Jersey: Prentice-Hall.

Maddox, R. (1995). *Inc. Your Dreams: For Any Woman Who is Thinking About Her own Business.* New York: Viking.

Mariotti, S. (1996). *The Young Entrepreneur's Guide to Starting and Running a Business.* New York: Times Books.

McConnell, C.R. & Brue, S.L. (1999). *Economics: Principles, Problems, and Policies* (14th ed.). New York: Irwin/McGraw-Hill.

Modu, E. (1996). *The Lemonade Stand: A Guide to Encouraging the Entrepreneur in Your Child.* Newark, New Jersey: Gateway Publisher.

National Foundation for Women Business Owners (NFWBO). (1996). "Women-Owned Businesses in the United States: 1996 Fact Sheets." Silver Spring, MD.

Reynolds, P.D. & White, S.B. (1997). *The Entrepreneurial Process: Economic Growth, Men, Women, and Minorities.* Quorum Books: Westport, Connecticut.

Timmons, J.A. (1990). *New Business Opportunities: Getting to the Right Place at the Right Time.* Acton, Massachusetts: Brick House Publishing.

Timmons, J.A. (1994). *New Venture Creation: Entrepreneurship for the 21st Century* (4th ed.). Boston, Massachusetts: Irwin.

U.S. Department of Commerce, Bureau of the Census. (1996a). "Women-Owned Business" (WB92-1). Washington, D.C.: U.S. Government Printing Office.

U.S. Department of Commerce, Bureau of the Census. (1996b). "Black-Owned Business" (MB92-1). Washington, D.C.: Bureau of the Census.

U.S. Department of Commerce. (1997). "Statistical Abstract of the United States." Washington, D.C.: U.S. Government Printing Office.

Walstad, W.B. (1994a). "Entrepreneurship and Small Business in the United States." Kansas City, Missouri: Center for Entrepreneurial Leadership Inc., Ewing Marion Kauffman Foundation.

Walstad, W.B. (1994b). *An International Perspective on Economic Education.* Boston: Kluwer Academic Publisher.

Walstad, W.B. (1996). "Youth and Entrepreneurship." Kansas City, Missouri: Center for Entrepreneurial Leadership Inc., Ewing Marion Kauffman Foundation.

Walstad, W.B. & Kourilsky, M.L. (1996). "The Findings From a National Survey of Entrepreneurship and Small Business." *Journal of Private Enterprise,* 11(2): 21-32.

Walstad, W.B. & Kourilsky, M.L. (forthcoming 1999). "Entrepreneurial Attitudes and Knowledge of Black Youth." *Entrepreneurship Theory and Practice.*

Zoghlin, G.G. (1991). *From Executive to Entrepreneur: Making the Transition.* New York: American Management Association.